Instructor's Guide

Medical Terminology:
An Anatomy and Physiology Systems Approach

Bonnie F. Fremgen, Ph.D.

Prentice Hall
Upper Saddle River, New Jersey 07458

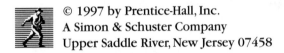
© 1997 by Prentice-Hall, Inc.
A Simon & Schuster Company
Upper Saddle River, New Jersey 07458

All rights reserved. No part of this book may be reproduced, in any form or by any means, without permission in writing from the publisher.

Printed in the United States of America
10 9 8 7 6 5 4 3

ISBN 0-8359-5060-3

Prentice-Hall International (UK) Limited, *London*
Prentice-Hall of Australia Pty. Limited, *Sydney*
Prentice-Hall Canada, Inc., *Toronto*
Prentice-Hall Hispanoamericana, S.A., *Mexico*
Prentice-Hall of India Private Limited, *New Delhi*
Prentice-Hall of Japan, Inc., *Tokyo*
Simon & Schuster Asia Pte. Ltd., *Singapore*
Editora Prentice-Hall do Brasil, Ltda., *Rio de Janeiro*

Introduction

This instructor's guide is prepared for instructors using *Medical Terminology: An Anatomy and Physiology Systems Approach*. The guide includes sample syllabi for using the text in both 16- and 10-week courses. Also included in the guide are test forms for quizzes, such as spelling and pronunciation tests, diagrams to assist the student in understanding anatomy and physiology, and methods to enhance learning medical terminology.

Sample Syllabus (16-Week Course, 48 Hours)

Week 1	Introduction to Medical Terminology	Chapter 1
Week 2	Body Structure	Chapter 2
Week 3	Integumentary System	Chapter 3
Week 4	Musculoskeletal System	Chapter 4
Week 5	Endocrine System	Chapter 5
Week 6	Cardiovascular System	Chapter 6
Week 7	Lymphatic and Hematic Systems	Chapter 7
Week 8	Midterm Examination	
Week 9	Respiratory System	Chapter 8
Week 10	Digestive System	Chapter 9
Week 11	Urinary System	Chapter 10
Week 12	Reproductive System	Chapter 11
Week 13	Nervous System	Chapter 12
Week 14	Special Senses: Eyes and Ears	Chapter 13
Week 15	Special Topics	Chapter 14
Week 16	Review	
Final Examination		

Sample Syllabus (10-Week Course, 40 Hours)

Week 1	Introduction to Medical Terminology	Chapter 1
Week 2	Body Structure	Chapter 2
	Integumentary System	Chapter 3
Week 3	Musculoskeletal System	Chapter 4
Week 4	Endocrine System	Chapter 5
	Cardiovascular System	Chapter 6

Week 5	Lymphatic and Hematic System	Chapter 7
	Respiratory System	Chapter 8
Week 6	Digestive System	Chapter 9
	Midterm Examination	
Week 7	Urinary System	Chapter 10
	Reproductive System	Chapter 11
Week 8	Nervous System	Chapter 12
Week 9	Special Senses: Eyes and Ears	Chapter 13
Week 10	Special Topics	Chapter 14
	Review	

Final Examination

LEARNING OBJECTIVES

Students should be able to complete all the learning objectives as a final chapter review. I have found that my students do much better in their course work when they complete the learning objectives as a turn-in assignment. These objectives may also be used as part of the final chapter examination.

This guide contains possible responses to the learning objectives. These are meant to be used as guidelines for the instructor. In some cases, the student responses may vary and still be correct.

STUDY HABITS

When mastering medical terminology, the student should be encouraged in the following study habits:

1. Take notes in an organized fashion. It is not enough just to listen to the instructor. Notes should be reviewed by the student on a daily basis. I always examined the students' notebooks to make sure that their note-taking skills were good. In some cases, a brief one-on-one session of skill building with the student was necessary.

   An example of one note-taking technique is provided subsequently. The note paper should be ruled with a large 2-inch margin on the left, which allows for key words and summaries. The 6.5 inches of the main paper on the right will contain all the lecture notes from class. Some students are able to do this in an outline form, whereas others may try to take down all the words of the instructor. Whatever method students use will benefit them because the mere exercise of writing down the material aids learning.

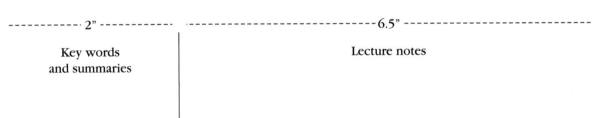

2. Work fast. Students must be encouraged to work fast when learning medical terminology. If a term is difficult to pronounce the first time, it will come much more easily with frequent practice. Students should avoid getting bogged down with memorizing terminology. If they repeat the words and definitions out loud, the learning progresses rapidly.

   I have found that students enjoy the opportunity to play verbal games in class to practice their pronunciation skills. In addition, writing the terms on the board as part of a relay team to practice correct spelling is an excellent exercise.

3. Work in small study groups outside of class to practice pronunciation and vocabulary.

4. Keep up with the reading! Medical terminology is like learning a foreign language. If a student gets behind in reading and study, especially during the first two chapters, it is difficult to catch up.
5. The student can tape the prefixes, suffixes, word roots, and their meanings onto audiotape. This tape can then be used by the student while they travel to and from classes to reinforce definitions.

FLASH CARDS

It is recommended that students prepare their own flash cards using index cards and felt-tip pens. The word root, prefix, or suffix is placed on one side of the card with the felt-tip pen, and the answer is placed on the back of the card in light pen or pencil. The students can use these cards to quiz themselves or when they meet in study groups. Once students have mastered these basic word parts, they can break apart most medical terms.

TESTING

Testing during every class period is recommended during the study of medical terminology. This is especially important during the study of the first few chapters of the textbook. The student must be able to grasp an understanding of word construction, word roots, suffixes, and prefixes.

This teacher's guide contains test forms that can be used in conjunction with teaching each chapter. For example, if the class is a 50-minute period three times a week, then a 5-minute quiz at the beginning of each class period will reinforce what was presented in the previous period. The students pick up the quiz as they enter the classroom and begin to do it without opening their books or talking. This is also an excellent way to get the class started.

The test forms in the guide can also be photocopied and distributed for use as study sheets.

Reinforcement of learning occurs when students correct the quizzes during class. Each student may be asked to provide the correct answer orally and mark the incorrect answer with colored pen.

Pronunciation and spelling tests for chapters 3 to 14 are encouraged. The instructor can select spelling terms from the lists of vocabulary terms provided in the guide. The spelling tests require the teacher to dictate the terms while the students write down the correct spelling. The audiotapes can also be used for spelling practice.

The teacher may wish to break up the class into relay teams for pronunciation practice. Written pronunciation tests require the students to break apart the medical terms into syllables with emphasis (underline) placed on the correct syllable.

AUDIOTAPE

The audiotape available with the textbook can be used several ways. Because the tape follows along with the text material (chapters 3 to 14), the students can play the tape after they have studied the chapter. Most of the medical terms listed in the vocabulary sections are included on the tape. If they term is a commonly used one (i.e., *heart, brain,* etc.), the word is not pronounced on the tape.

In addition, the tapes can be used in the classroom with all the students pronouncing the terms as a group.

CLASSROOM ACTIVITIES

Occasional breaks during the class session can be beneficial. Have the students stand up and assume the anatomic position, and show the directional terms as you indicate directions, such as *ventral, dorsal, proximal,* and *distal.*

While in the anatomic position, a student spokesperson can give directions including the following:

- Flex the right leg
- Extend the right leg
- Dorsiflex the right foot
- Pronate the left hand
- Supinate the right hand

BOARD WORK

I have found that one of the most effective learning methods for students is for them to "teach" the class by using the board. This can be done by having students use the board to outline the organs within each system, spell difficult terms, and identify organs on model outlines the teacher has placed on the board.

ABBREVIATIONS

Students need reinforcement in learning abbreviations. The text contains abbreviations related to each system at the end of the chapter and a complete list of abbreviations in the appendix. However, because the medical world is a world of abbreviations, the students must be comfortable in using the correct ones and not form their own abbreviations.

MEDICAL DICTIONARY

The practice exercises in the textbook can be completed without the use of a medical dictionary. However, a medical terminology course can be the perfect vehicle for the introduction of dictionary use.

Many end-of-chapter case studies in the textbook contain terms that lead to medical dictionary work on the part of the student.

1
Introduction to Medical Terminology

Learning Objectives

1. Discuss the four parts to medical terms.
   a. *Word root.* The main part or fundamental meaning of the word.
   b. *Prefix.* A short term added in front of the word root that clarifies the term.
   c. *Combining form.* A vowel added between word roots, or a word root and a suffix to ease the pronunciation of the term. The combining vowel *o* is generally used. A combining vowel is not used if the suffix begins with a vowel.
   d. *Suffix.* A short term or word attached to the end of a word root to provide additional meaning to the word.
2. Correct spelling is vital in using medical terminology. Pronunciation of a term may vary slightly depending on the geographic area or medical discipline, but spelling never varies.
3. Recognize word roots and the combining vowel/form.

   Note. You may wish to use Test 1A to assist in determining if students have gained this knowledge.

	Word Root	Meaning
1.	gastr/o	stomach
2.	encephal/o	brain
3.	hem/o	blood
4.	cyst/o	bladder
5.	enter/o	intestines
6.	cardi/o	heart
7.	hepat/o	liver
8.	hyster/o	uterus
9.	aden/o	gland
10.	col/o	colon
11.	arthr/o	joint
12.	dermat/o	skin
13.	cephal/o	head
14.	esophag/o	esophagus
15.	carcin/o	cancer
16.	cerebr/o	cerebrum

	Word Root	Meaning
17.	gloss/o	tongue
18.	ile/o	ileum of small intestine
19.	nephr/o	kidney
20.	ped/o	child
21.	thromb/o	clot
22.	cyt/o	cell
23.	gynec/o	female
24.	erythr/o	red
25.	hemat/o	blood
26.	lingu/o	tongue
27.	ren/o	kidney
28.	oste/o	bone
29.	neur/o	nerve
30.	ur/o	urinary tract
31.	rhin/o	nose
32.	pharyng/o	pharynx
33.	ot/o	ear
34.	leuk/o	white
35.	splen/o	spleen
36.	path/o	disease
37.	trache/o	trachea
38.	derm/o	skin
39.	onc/o	tumor
40.	ophthalm/o	eye
41.	rect/o	rectum
42.	cholecyst/o	gallbladder

4. Identify the most important prefixes and suffixes.

   Note. You may wish to administer Tests 1B and 1C to your students to determine if they can correctly identify prefixes and suffixes.

	Prefix	Meaning
1.	a-	without/away from
2.	ab-	away from/negative/absent
3.	ad-	toward/in the direction
4.	ambi-	both/both sides
5.	an-	without
6.	ante-	before/in front of
7.	anter/o	before/in front of
8.	ar-	without
9.	auto-	self
10.	bi-	two
11.	brady-	slow
12.	circum-	around
13.	contra-	against
14.	dextr/o	to the right of
15.	dia-	through/across
16.	diplo-	double
17.	dors/o	back
18.	dys-	painful/difficult
19.	ec-	out/out from
20.	endo-	within
21.	epi-	on

INSTRUCTOR'S GUIDE   MEDICAL TERMINOLOGY

	Prefix	Meaning
22.	ex-	out from
23.	exo-	out
24.	hemi-	half
25.	heter/o	different
26.	homo-	same
27.	hydro-	water
28.	hyper-	over/above
29.	hypo-	under/below
30.	im-	not
31.	in-	not/into
32.	infra-	under/beneath/ below
33.	inter-	among/between
34.	intra-	within/inside
35.	later/o	side
36.	leuk/o	white
37.	macr/o	large
38.	mal-	bad/ill
39.	medi-	middle
40.	mes/o	middle
41.	micro-	small
42.	mid-	middle
43.	pan-	all
44.	peri-	around
45.	poly-	many/much
46.	post-	after
47.	postero-	after/behind
48.	pre-	before/in front of
49.	pro-	before/in front of
50.	pseudo-	false
51.	re-	back
52.	retro-	after/behind
53.	sinistro-	left
54.	sub-	below/under
55.	super-	above
56.	supra-	above
57.	syn-	together
58.	tachy-	rapid/fast
59.	trans-	through/across
60.	ultra-	beyond/excess
61.	di-	two
62.	mono-	one
63.	multi-	many
64.	semi-	partial
65.	tri-	three
66.	quad-	four
67.	alb-	white, protein
68.	albumin-	white
69.	chlor/o-	green
70.	cirrh/o-	yellow
71.	cyan/o-	blue
72.	erythr/o-	red
73.	melan/o-	black
74.	purpur/o-	purple
75.	rube/o-	red

	Suffix	Meaning
1.	-ac	pertaining or relating to
2.	-al	pertaining or relating to
3.	-algia	pertaining to pain
4.	-cele	swelling/hernia
5.	-centesis	surgical puncture to remove fluid
6.	-cide	kill
7.	-cise	cut
8.	-cle	small
9.	-cyte	cell
10.	-dyne	pain
11.	-ectasis	dilation
12.	-ectomy	surgical removal of
13.	-ectopy	displacement
14.	-emia	condition of the blood
15.	-genic	produced by
16.	-gram	record or picture (instrument)
17.	-graph	record or picture
18.	-graphy	recording a record or picture
19.	-ia	pertaining to
20.	-iasis	presence of
21.	-ic	pertaining to
22.	-id	condition of
23.	-ion	small
24.	-itis	inflammation
25.	-ium	small
26.	-ize	remove/take away
27.	-lith	stone
28.	-lysis	destruction
29.	-malacia	abnormal softening
30.	-megaly	enlargement or large
31.	-oid	resembling
32.	-ology	study of
33.	-ostomy	surgically create an opening
34.	-otomy	cutting into
35.	-parous	bearing/giving birth
36.	-pathy	disease
37.	-penia	few
38.	-pexy	fixation
39.	-phasia	speech
40.	-phobia	abnormal fear
41.	-plasty	surgical repair
42.	-pnea	breathing
43.	-ptosis	drooping/dropping of an organ
44.	-rrhage	excessive/abnormal flow
45.	-rrhea	discharge or flow
46.	-rrhexis	rupture
47.	-scopy	to visualize (usually with equipment)
48.	-sis	state of
49.	-spasm	twitch/involuntary muscle movement
50.	-stalsis	constriction/contracture
51.	-stenosis	abnormal narrowing or stricture
52.	-trophy	nourishment
53.	-uria	pertaining to the urine removal

5. Word building is putting together several parts of a word to form a medical term. The combining form of a word root may be added to another word root along with a prefix or a suffix to form a new word.
6. *Recognizing Abbreviations*: Students must be aware that there can be multiple meanings for an abbreviation. The example of SM for simple mastectomy and sm for small is discussed in chapter 1. Other examples might include the following:

Abbreviation	Multiple Meaning
BS	breath sounds or bowel sounds
Ca	calcium or cancer
ERT	estrogen replacement therapy or external radiation therapy
HD	hemodialysis or Hodgkin's disease
MI	myocardial infarction or mitral insufficiency
mono	mononucleosis or monocyte
MS	musculoskeletal, multiple sclerosis or mitral stenosis
PAP	pulmonary arterial pressure or Papanicolaou (Pap) test
PEG	percutaneous endoscopic gastrostomy or pneumoencephalogram
R	respiratory or roentgen
RML	right middle lobe or right mediolateral
SG	specific gravity or skin graft

Name _____ Date _____ Errors _____

Test 1A Word Roots With Combining Form

Write the definition of the word root/combining form in the space provided.

	Word Root	**Definition**
1.	gastr/o	
2.	encephal/o	
3.	hem/o	
4.	cyst/o	
5.	enter/o	
6.	cardi/o	
7.	hepat/o	
8.	hyster/o	
9.	aden/o	
10.	col/o	
11.	arthr/o	
12.	dermat/o	
13.	cephal/o	
14.	esophag/o	
15.	carcin/o	
16.	cerebr/o	
17.	gloss/o	
18.	ile/o	
19.	nephr/o	
20.	ped/o	
21.	thromb/o	
22.	cyt/o	
23.	gynec/o	
24.	erythr/o	
25.	hemat/o	
26.	lingu/o	
27.	ren/o	
28.	oste/o	

	Word Root	Definition
29.	neur/o	
30.	ur/o	
31.	rhin/o	
32.	pharyng/o	
33.	ot/o	
34.	leuk/o	
35.	splen/o	
36.	path/o	
37.	trache/o	
38.	derm/o	
39.	onc/o	
40.	ophthalm/o	
41.	rect/o	
42.	cholecyst/o	

Name _____ Date _____ Errors _____

Test 1B Identifying Prefixes

Write the meaning next to each prefix. In some cases, the prefix and combining vowel will be given (i.e., anter/o).

1. a- _____
2. ab- _____
3. ad- _____
4. ambi- _____
5. an- _____
6. ante- _____
7. anter/o _____
8. ar- _____
9. auto- _____
10. bi- _____
11. brady- _____
12. circum- _____
13. contra- _____
14. dextr/o _____
15. dia- _____
16. diplo- _____
17. dors/o _____
18. dys- _____
19. ec- _____
20. endo- _____
21. epi- _____
22. ex- _____
23. exo- _____
24. hemi- _____
25. heter/o _____
26. homo- _____
27. hydro- _____
28. hyper- _____
29. hypo- _____

30. im- _____
31. in- _____
32. infra- _____
33. inter- _____
34. intra- _____
35. later/o _____
36. leuk/o _____
37. macr/o _____
38. mal- _____
39. medi- _____
40. mes/o _____
41. micro- _____
42. mid- _____
43. pan- _____
44. peri- _____
45. poly- _____
46. post- _____
47. postero- _____
48. pre- _____
49. pro- _____
50. pseudo- _____
51. re- _____
52. retro- _____
53. sinistro- _____
54. sub- _____
55. super- _____
56. supra- _____
57. syn- _____
58. tachy- _____
59. trans- _____
60. ultra- _____
61. di- _____
62. mono- _____
63. multi- _____

64. semi- _____
65. tri- _____
66. quad- _____
67. alb- _____
68. albumin- _____
69. chlor/o- _____
70. cirrh/o- _____
71. cyan/o- _____
72. erythr/o- _____
73. melan/o- _____
74. purpur/o- _____
75. rube/o- _____

Name _____ Date _____ Errors _____

Test 1C   Identifying Suffixes

Write the meaning next to each suffix.

1. -ac _____
2. -al _____
3. -algia _____
4. -cele _____
5. -centesis _____
6. -cide _____
7. -cise _____
8. -cle _____
9. -cyte _____
10. -dyne _____
11. -ectasis _____
12. -ectomy _____
13. -ectopy _____
14. -emia _____
15. -genic _____
16. -gram _____
17. -graph _____
18. -graphy _____
19. -ia _____
20. -iasis _____
21. -ic _____
22. -id _____
23. -ion _____
24. -itis _____
25. -ium _____
26. -ize _____
27. -lith _____
28. -lysis _____
29. -malacia _____

12   INSTRUCTOR'S GUIDE   MEDICAL TERMINOLOGY

30. -megaly
31. -oid
32. -ology
33. -ostomy
34. -otomy
35. -parous
36. -pathy
37. -penia
38. -pexy
39. -phasia
40. -phobia
41. -plasty
42. -pnea
43. -ptosis
44. -rrhage
45. -rrhea
46. -rrhexis
47. -scopy
48. -sis
49. -spasm
50. -stalsis
51. -stenosis
52. -trophy
53. -uria

2

Body Structure

Learning Objectives

1. Recognize the combining forms used in this chapter.

    Note. You may wish to use Test 2A to assist in determining if the student has gained this knowledge.

	Word Root	Meaning
1.	abdomin/o	abdomen
2.	lumb/o	lower back
3.	anter/o	front
4.	medi/o	middle
5.	cephal/o	head
6.	my/o	muscle
7.	cervic/o	neck
8.	pelv/o	hip, pelvic
9.	chrondr/o	cartilage
10.	poster/o	back
11.	coccyg/o	coccyx
12.	proxim/o	near
13.	crani/o	skull
14.	sacr/o	sacrum
15.	cyt/o	cell
16.	system/o	system
17.	dors/o	back of body
18.	spin/o	spine, backbone
19.	epithele/o	epithelium
20.	thorax/o	chest
21.	hist/o	tissue
22.	umbilic/o	naval
23.	ili/o	ilium (pelvic bone)
24.	ventr/o	belly
25.	later/o	side
26.	vertebra/o	vertebra
27.	viscer/o	internal organ

2. Discuss the organization of the body in terms of cells, tissues, organs, and systems.

   The basic unit of all living things is the cell, which forms the tissues and organs of the body. The organism (human body) is the sum total of all the body systems.

3. Define the following four types of tissues:
   a. *Muscle tissue.* This is composed of both voluntary and involuntary tissue and produces movement within the body.
   b. *Epithelial tissue.* This tissue, found throughout the body, lines internal organs and also acts as a covering or skin.
   c. *Mucous tissue.* Mucous membranes are a type of epithelial tissue found lining body surfaces.
   d. *Connective tissue.* This tissue supports and protects the tissue in body structures.

4. List the organs found in the 11 organ systems.

   Note. You may wish to use Test 2B to assess students' knowledge.

	Body System		**Organs in the System**
1.	integumentary	a.	skin
		b.	sweat glands
		c.	sebaceous glands
		d.	hair
		e.	nails
2.	musculoskeletal	a.	muscles
		b.	tendons
		c.	bones
		d.	joints
		e.	cartilage
3.	endocrine	a.	thyroid
		b.	pituitary
		c.	testes
		d.	ovaries
		e.	adrenal
		f.	pancreas
		g.	pineal
		h.	thymus
4.	cardiovascular	a.	heart
		b.	arteries
		c.	veins
5.	lymphatic and hematic	a.	spleen
		b.	lymph
		c.	white blood cells
6.	respiratory	a.	nose
		b.	pharynx
		c.	larynx
		d.	trachea
		e.	lungs
		f.	bronchial tubes

	Body System	**Organs in the System**
7.	gastrointestinal	a. mouth b. pharynx c. esophagus d. stomach e. small intestine f. large intestine g. liver h. gallbladder i. anus
8.	urinary	a. kidneys b. ureters c. bladder d. urethra
9.	reproductive	a. ovaries b. uterus c. vagina d. mammary e. testes f. prostate g. urethra h. anus
10.	nervous	a. brain b. spinal cord c. nerves
11.	special senses	a. eye b. ear

5. Define the anatomical position

   The anatomical position describes the body when it is erect, with arms at the sides, palms of the hands facing forward, and the eyes straight ahead. For descriptive purposes, the assumption is always that the person is in the anatomical position.

6. Discuss the body planes.

   Note. You may wish to have students identify the body planes on Test 2C.

7. Define the directional terms.

   Note: You may wish to use Test 2D to test knowledge of the directional terms.

	Directional Term	**Defintion**
1.	superior (cephalic)	toward the head
2.	inferior (caudal)	toward the feet
3.	anterior (ventral)	near the front
4.	posterior (dorsal)	near the back
5.	medial	on or near the middle
6.	lateral	toward the side

	Directional Term	Defintion
7.	apex	at the tip or summit
8.	base	toward the bottom
9.	abduction	to move away from
10.	adduction	to move toward
11.	proximal	located nearest the center
12.	distal	located away from the center
13.	superficial	toward the surface
14.	deep	away from the surface
15.	supine	lying horizontal, facing up
16.	prone	lying horizontal, facing down
17.	parietal	wall of an organ
18.	visceral	covering or surface of the body or organ
19.	inversion	to turn inward
20.	eversion	to turn outward

8. Locate and describe the nine regions of the abdominal area.

   Note. You may wish to have students identify the nine regions of the abdominal areas in Test 2E.

9. State and define the four quadrants of the abdominopelvic area.

   The four quadrants are the following:

   a. The right upper quadrant (RUQ) containing the right lobe of the liver, gallbladder, portion of the pancreas, and portion of small and large intestine.

   b. The right lower quadrant (RLQ) containing portions of the small and large intestines, right ovary and fallopian tube, appendix, and right ureter.

   c. The left upper quadrant (LUQ) containing the left lobe of the liver, spleen, stomach, portion of the pancreas, and portion of small and large intestines.

   d. The left lower quadrant (LLQ) containing portions of the small and large intestines, left ovary and fallopian tube, and left ureter.

   Identify the most important prefixes and suffixes discussed within the chapter.

   Note. You may wish to administer Test 2F to your students to determine if they can correctly identify prefixes and suffixes.

	Prefix	Meaning
1.	contra-	against
2.	epi-	above
3.	ex-	away from
4.	inter-	between
5.	intra-	within
6.	peri-	around
7.	post-	behind/after
8.	retro-	backward
9.	semi-	half
10.	sub-	under/below
11.	supra-	above
12.	trans-	through/across
13.	tri-	three

	Suffix	Meaning
1.	-ac	pertaining to
2.	-al	pertaining to
3.	-ar	pertaining to
4.	-ary	pertaining to
5.	-ectomy	surgical removal
6.	-ic	pertaining to
7.	-plasm	formation

ABBREVIATIONS

Note: You may wish to use Test 2G to test students' knowledge of abbreviations relating to body structure.

	Abbreviation	Meaning
1.	AP	antero-posterior
2.	UGI	upper gastrointestinal
3.	CNS	central nervous system
4.	RUQ	right upper quadrant
5.	CV	cardiovascular
6.	RLQ	right lower quadrant
7.	GB	gallbladder
8.	PNS	peripheral nervous system
9.	GI	gastrointestinal
10.	MS	musculoskeletal
11.	GU	genitourinary
12.	LUQ	left upper quadrant
13.	lat	lateral
14.	LLQ	left lower quadrant
15.	LB	large bowel
16.	LK&S	liver, kidney, and spleen

Name _____ Date _____ Errors _____

Test 2A   Word Roots with Combining Form for Body Structure

Define the word root/combining form in the space provided next to each term.

	Word Root	Meaning
1.	abdomin/o	
2.	lumb/o	
3.	anter/o	
4.	medi/o	
5.	cephal/o	
6.	my/o	
7.	cervic/o	
8.	pelv/o	
9.	chrondr/o	
10.	poster/o	
11.	coccyg/o	
12.	proxim/o	
13.	crani/o	
14.	sacr/o	
15.	cyt/o	
16.	system/o	
17.	dors/o	
18.	spin/o	
19.	epithele/o	
20.	thorax/o	
21.	hist/o	
22.	umbilic/o	
23.	ili/o	
24.	ventr/o	
25.	later/o	
26.	vertebra/o	
27.	viscer/o	

Name _____ Date _____ Errors _____

Test 2B   Defining Body Systems

Place the names of the organs that are included within each body system in the spaces provided.

	Body System		Organs in the System
1.	integumentary	a.	_____
		b.	_____
		c.	_____
		d.	_____
		e.	_____
2.	musculoskeletal	a.	_____
		b.	_____
		c.	_____
		d.	_____
		e.	_____
3.	endocrine	a.	_____
		b.	_____
		c.	_____
		d.	_____
		e.	_____
		f.	_____
		g.	_____
		h.	_____
4.	cardiovascular	a.	_____
		b.	_____
		c.	_____
5.	lymphatic and hematic	a.	_____
		b.	_____
		c.	_____
6.	respiratory	a.	_____
		b.	_____
		c.	_____
		d.	_____
		e.	_____
		f.	_____

	Body System		**Organs in the System**
7.	gastrointestinal	a.	_____
		b.	_____
		c.	_____
		d.	_____
		e.	_____
		f.	_____
		g.	_____
		h.	_____
		i.	_____
8.	urinary	a.	_____
		b.	_____
		c.	_____
		d.	_____
9.	reproductive	a.	_____
		b.	_____
		c.	_____
		d.	_____
		e.	_____
		f.	_____
		g.	_____
		h.	_____
10.	nervous	a.	_____
		b.	_____
		c.	_____
11.	special senses	a.	_____
		b.	_____

Name _____ Date _____ Errors _____

Test 2C   Identifying the Anatomical Planes

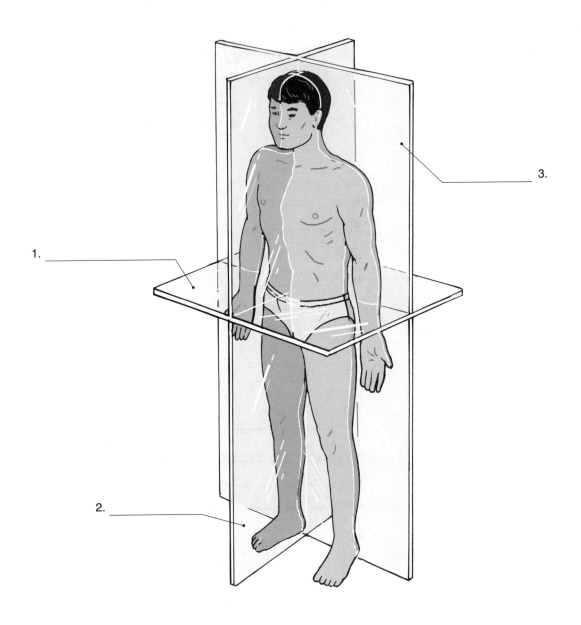

1. _____
2. _____
3. _____

Name _____ Date _____ Errors _____

Test 2C   Instructor's Answers: Anatomical Planes

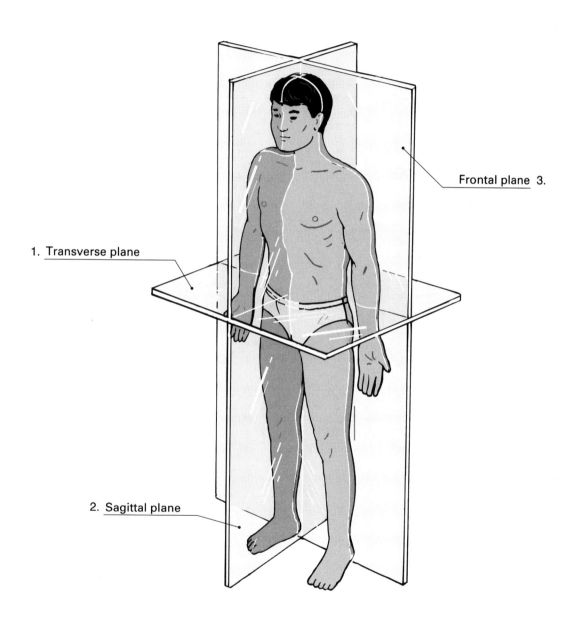

Chapter 2   Body Structure   **25**

Name _____ Date _____ Errors _____

Test 2D Directional Terms

Place the definition/description of the directional position in the space next to the term.

    Directional   **Term Defintion**

1. superior (cephalic) _____
2. inferior (caudal) _____
3. anterior (ventral) _____
4. posterior (dorsal) _____
5. medial _____
6. lateral _____
7. apex _____
8. base _____
9. abduction _____
10. adduction _____
11. proximal _____
12. distal _____
13. superficial _____
14. deep _____
15. supine _____
16. prone _____
17. parietal _____
18. visceral _____
19. inversion _____
20. eversion _____

Name _____ Date _____ Errors _____

Test 2E Identifying the Nine Abdominal Regions

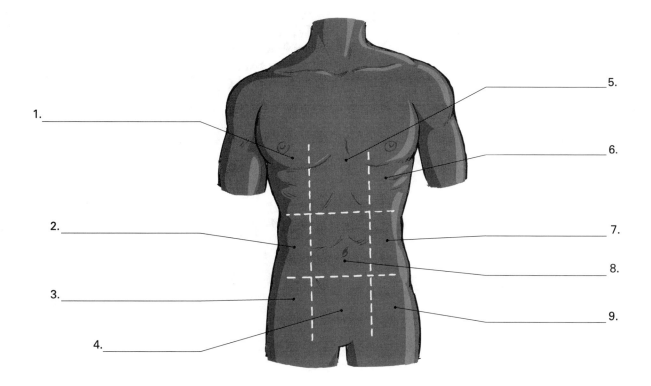

1. _____
2. _____
3. _____
4. _____
5. _____
6. _____
7. _____
8. _____
9. _____

Chapter 2 Body Structure **27**

Name _____ Date _____ Errors _____

Test 2E Instructor's Answers: Nine Abdominal Regions

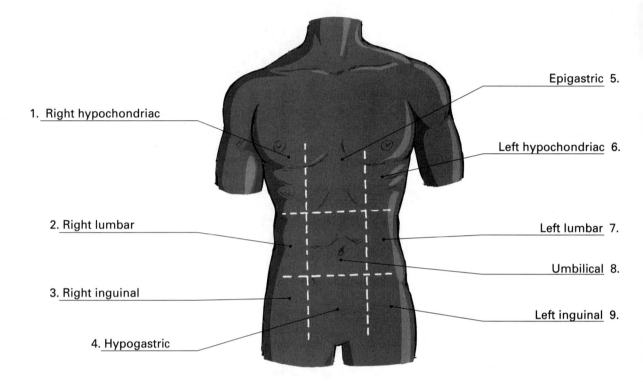

1. Right hypochondriac
2. Right lumbar
3. Right inguinal
4. Hypogastric
5. Epigastric
6. Left hypochondriac
7. Left lumbar
8. Umbilical
9. Left inguinal

Name _____ Date _____ Errors _____

Test 2F Identifying Prefixes and Suffixes

Place the meaning of the term in the space provided.

	Prefix	**Meaning**
1.	contra-	
2.	epi-	
3.	ex-	
4.	inter-	
5.	intra-	
6.	peri-	
7.	post-	
8.	retro-	
9.	semi-	
10.	sub-	
11.	supra-	
12.	trans-	
13.	tri-	

	Suffix	**Meaning**
1.	-ac	
2.	-al	
3.	-ar	
4.	-ary	
5.	-ectomy	
6.	-ic	
7.	-plasm	

Name _____ Date _____ Errors _____

Test 2G Abbreviations for the Body Structure

Write the meaning of the abbreviation in the space provided.

	Abbreviation	**Meaning**
1.	AP	_____
2.	UGI	_____
3.	CNS	_____
4.	RUQ	_____
5.	CV	_____
6.	RLQ	_____
7.	GB	_____
8.	PNS	_____
9.	GI	_____
10.	MS	_____
11.	GU	_____
12.	LUQ	_____
13.	lat	_____
14.	LLQ	_____
15.	LB	_____
16.	LK&S	_____

3

Integumentary System

Learning Objectives

1. Identify the word roots and combining forms relating to the integumentary system.

    Note. You many wish to use Test 3A to assist in determining if the student has gained this knowledge.

	Word Root	**Meaning**
1.	onych/o	nail
2.	albin/o	white
3.	cry/o	cold
4.	cutane/o	skin
5.	chrom/o	color
6.	papul/o	pimple
7.	pil/o	hair
8.	melan/o	black
9.	trich/o	hair
10.	cyan/o	blue
11.	py/o	pus
12.	macul/o	stain/spot
13.	xer/o	dry
14.	derm/o	skin
15.	lip/o	fat
16.	vit/o	blemish
17.	dermat/o	skin
18.	leuk/o	white
19.	rhytid/o	wrinkle
20.	erythem/o	flush
21.	scler/o	hard
22.	kerat/o	hard/horny
23.	vesic/o	blister
24.	hidr/o	sweat
25.	seb/o	sebum, oil
26.	hist/o	tissue
27.	ungu/o	nail
28.	histi/o	tissue

2. List the major organs of this system.

   Note. You may wish to use Test 3B to test the students' knowledge.

3. Describe the four purposes of the skin:
   a. protecting internal organs
   b. housing nerve receptors (temperature, pain, touch, and pressure)
   c. secreting fluids (sweat and sebaceous)
   d. regulating temperature

4. Discuss the structure and function of the three layers of the skin.

   Note. You may wish to use Test 3C to test students' knowledge.

5. List and describe the accessory organs of the skin.
   a. hair
   b. nails
   c. sebaceous glands
   d. sweat glands

6. Discuss the following three classifications of burns:
   a. *First degree.* Involves superficial outer layer of epidermis
   b. *Second degree.* Damage through the epidermis and into the dermis causing vesicles to form
   c. *Third degree.* Damage to full thickness of epidermis and dermis with fluid loss and scarring

7. List and describe eight common skin lesions.

   Note. You may wish to use Test 3D to assess student's knowledge.

8. Recognize descriptions of skin infections.

   Skin Infection Description

a.	boil	Inflammation of subcutaneous layer of skin, gland, or hair follicle. Also called furuncle.
b.	carbuncle	Infection of skin and hair follicle from untreated boils.
c.	furuncle	Staphylococcal (staph) skin abscess with redness, pain, and swelling. Also called a boil.
d.	impetigo	Inflammatory skin disease with pustules that crust and rupture.
e.	sebaceous cyst	Cyst filled with sebum.
f.	scabies	Contagious skin disease caused by a mite.
g.	tinea	Fungal skin disease.
h.	verruca	Benign neoplasm caused by a virus. Also called warts.

9. State the terminology for four benign and four malignant neoplasms.

   Benign Neoplasms

   a. *Dermatofibroma.* Fibrous skin tumor
   b. *Hemangioma.* Tumor of dilated blood vessels
   c. *Keloid.* Scar left after injury or surgery
   d. *Keratosis.* Thickening of epithelium
   e. *Leukoplakia.* White patches in mucous membrane

f. *Lipoma*. Fatty tumor

g. *Nevus*. Pigmented congenital skin blemish

Malignant Neoplasms

a. *Basal cell carcinoma*. Epithelial tumor of basal cell layer that rarely metastasizes

b. *Kaposi's sarcoma*. Skin cancer seen in acquired immune deficiency syndrome (AIDS) patients consisting of brownish-purple patches

c. *Malignant melanoma*. Cancer caused by overgrowth of melanin that may metastasize

d. *Squamous cell carcinoma*. Epidermal cancer that does not generally metastasize

10. Recognize vocabulary terms for the integumentary system.

    Note. You may wish to test the student on the following terms:

depigmentation	diaphoresis	ecchymosis
erythema	frostbite	hirsutism
hyperpigmentation	acne	alopecia
dermatitis	dermatographia	gangrene
keratosis	leukoderma	leukoplakia
nevus	onychia	pachyderma
paronychia	pediculosis	pemphigus vulgaris
petechiae	photosensitivity	purpura
pruritus	seborrhea	shingles
ulcer	vitiligo	xeroderma
abrasion	adipectomy	cauterization
cellulitis	chemobrasion	cryosurgery
curettage	debridement	dermabrasion
dermatome	dermatoplasty	electrocautery
laser therapy	lipectomy	liposuction
marsupialization	needle biopsy	plication
rhytidectomy	skin graft	biopsy
frozen section	fungal scrapings	skin tests
sweat test		
exfoliative cytology		
incision and drainage		
systemic lupus erythematosis		

    Note. The preceding list may also be used to test dictation skills and spelling.

11. Correctly identify the terms for color.

	Term	Meaning
a.	cyan/o	blue
b.	melan/o	black
c.	poli/o	gray
d.	chlor/o	green
e.	cirrh/o	yellow/orange
f.	rose/o	pink
g.	purpur/a	purple
h.	eryth/o	red
i.	rube/o	red
j.	rose/o	rose

Pronunciation Guide: Integumentary System

Vocabulary

depigmentation (de pig men TA shun)
diaphoresis (di a fore RE sis)
ecchymosis (ek e MO sis)
erythema (er ah THE ma)
hirsutism (HER su tizm)

Common Disorders of the Integumentary System

acne (AK ne)
alopecia (al oh PEE sheah)
dermatitis (der ma TI tis)
dermatographia (der ma to GRAF ee ah)
gangrene (GANG green)
keratosis (ker ah TOE sis)
leukoderma (loo ko DER ma)
leukoplakia (loo ko PLAY key ah)
nevus (NE vus)
onychia (oh NIK ee ah)
paronychia (par oh NIK ee ah)
pediculosis (pe dik u LO sis)
pemphigus vulgaris (PEM fi gus/ vul GARE is)
petechiae (pe TEA key eye)
purpura (PURR pu ra)
pruritus (pru RI tus)
seborrhea (seb or EE ah)
shingles (SHING lz)
systemic lupus erythematosus (systemic/ lupus/ er eh the ma TOE sis)
ulcer (UL sir)
vitiligo (vit il EYE go)

Skin Infections

carbuncle (car BUNG kl)
furuncle (FUR un cle)
impetigo (im pee TIE go)
sebaceous cyst (se BA shus/ cyst)
scabies (SKA bees)
tinea (TIN ee ah)
verruca (Ver ROO ka)

Inflammatory Skin Disorders

cellulitis (sel u LI tis)
decubitus (de KU bi tus)
eczema (EK sima)
psoriasis (so RYE ah sis)
scleroderma (sclir oh DER ma)
urticaria (ur ti CARE ee ah)

Skin Neoplasms

dermatofibroma (der ma toe fi BRO ma)
hemangioma (he man je OH ma)
keloid (KEY loid)
keratosis (KER ah tow sis)
leukoplakia (loo co PLAY key ah)
lipoma (LIE po ma)
nevus (KNEE vus)
basal cell carcinoma (basal/ cell/ kar sin NO ma)
Kaposi's sarcoma (KAP oh sez/ sar KO ma)
malignant melanoma (malignant/ MEL an oh ma)
squamous (SKWA mus)

Terminology Related to Procedures

abrasion (ah BRAY shun)
adipectomy (ad eh PECK toe me)
cauterization (kaw tur eh ZAY shun)
cellulitis (sel u LI tis)
chemobrasion (keem oh BRAY shun)
cryosurgery (CRY oh surg er ee)
curettage (ku re TAZH)
debridement (da bred MON)
dermabrasion (der ma BRAY shun)
dermatome (DER ma tom)
dermatoplasty (DER mat oh plas te)
electrocautery (elec TRO kaw tur ee)
exfoliative cytology (ex FOE lee ah tive/ sigh TOL oh gee)
lipectomy (lie PECK toe me)
liposuction (LIP oh suck shun)
marsupialization (mar sue pee al ih ZAY shun)
plication (ply KAY shun)
rhytidectomy (rit eh DECK tow me)

Diagnostic and Laboratory Tests

biopsy (BYE op see)
fungal scrapings (FUN gal/ scrapings)

Spelling Test

Note. You may wish to use the Spelling Test Form in this manual to test students' knowledge. Select any of the above vocabulary terms.

Abbreviations

Note. You may wish to use Test 3E to test students' knowledge of abbreviations relating to the integumentary system.

	Abbreviation	Meaning
1.	BX	biopsy
2.	Derm	dermatology
3.	FS	frozen section
4.	H	hypodermic
5.	I&D	incision and drainage
6.	ID	intradermal
7.	LE	lupus erythematosis
8.	SCLE	subacute cutaneous lupus erythematosis
9.	SG	skin graft
10.	STSG	split-thickness skin graft
11.	SLE	systemic lupus erythematosis
12.	STD	skin test done
13.	Subcu	subcutaneous
14.	Subq	subcutaneous
15.	UV	ultraviolet
16.	ung	ointment

Name _____ Date _____ Errors _____

Test 3A Identifying Word Roots with Combining Form

Write the definition of the word root in the space provided.

	Word Root	Meaning
1.	onych/o	
2.	albin/o	
3.	cry/o	
4.	cutane/o	
5.	chrom/o	
6.	papul/o	
7.	pil/o	
8.	melan/o	
9.	trich/o	
10.	cyan/o	
11.	py/o	
12.	macul/o	
13.	xer/o	
14.	derm/o	
15.	lip/o	
16.	vit/o	
17.	dermat/o	
18.	leuk/o	
19.	rhytid/o	
20.	erythem/o	
21.	scler/o	
22.	kerat/o	
23.	vesic/o	
24.	hidr/o	
25.	seb/o	
26.	hist/o	
27.	ungu/o	
28.	histi/o	

Name _____ Date _____ Errors _____

Test 3B   Identifying the Organs of the Integumentary System

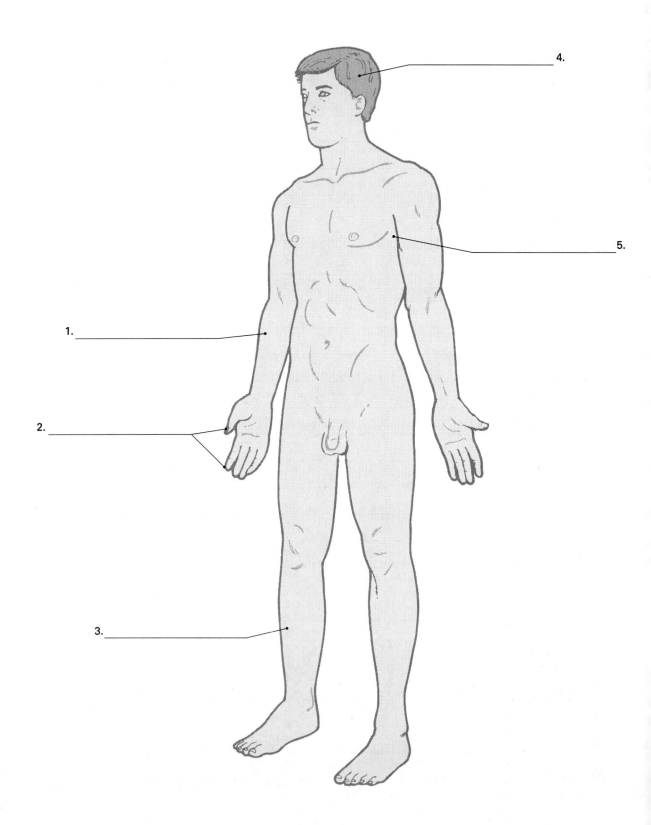

1. _____
2. _____
3. _____
4. _____
5. _____

Name _____ Date _____ Errors _____

Test 3B   Instructor's Answers: Organs of the Integumentary System

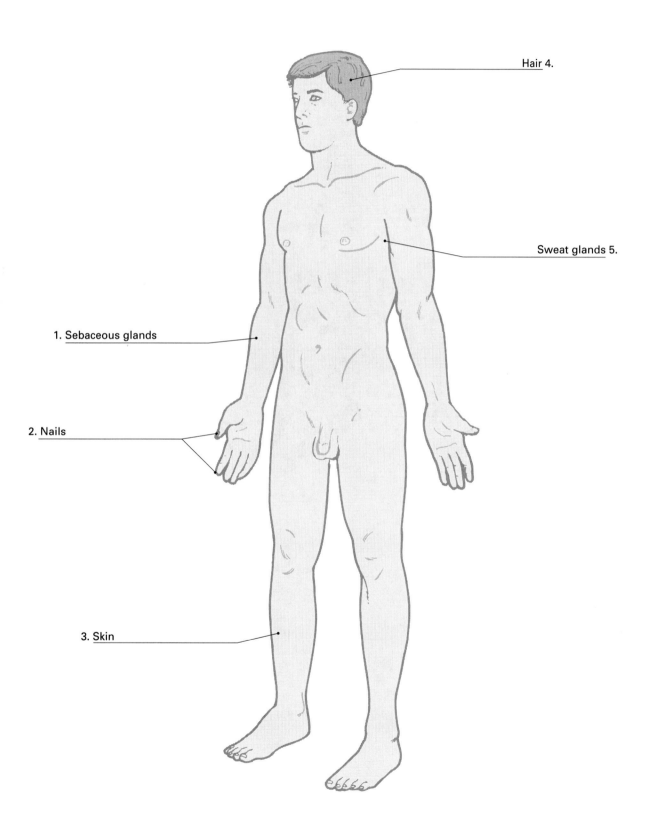

Chapter 3   Integumentary System   **39**

Name _____ Date _____ Errors _____

Test 3C   Identifying the Components of the Skin

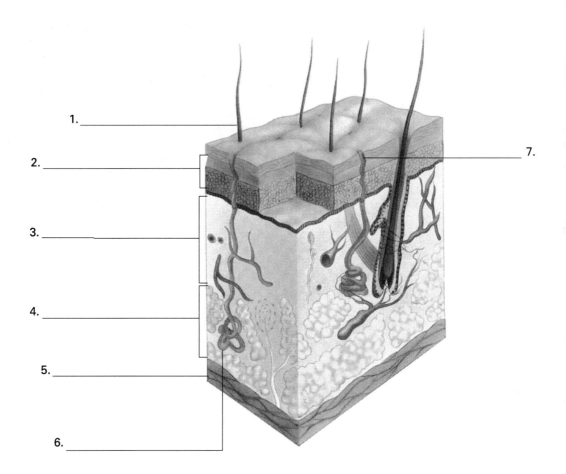

1. _____
2. _____
3. _____
4. _____
5. _____
6. _____
7. _____

Name _____ Date _____ Errors _____

Test 3C   Instructor's Answers: Components of the Skin

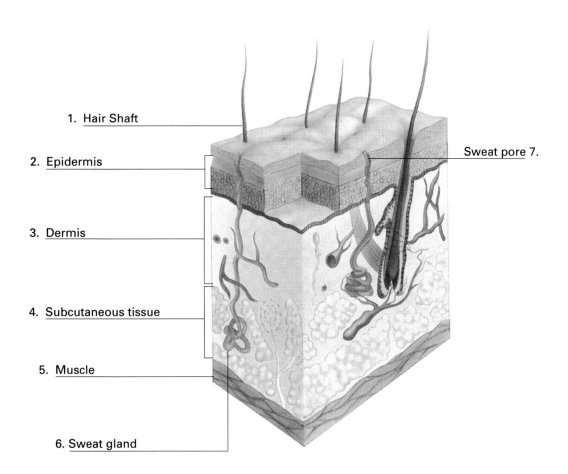

1. Hair Shaft
2. Epidermis
3. Dermis
4. Subcutaneous tissue
5. Muscle
6. Sweat gland

Sweat pore 7.

Chapter 3   Integumentary System   **41**

Name _____ Date _____ Errors _____

Test 3D   Common Skin Lesions

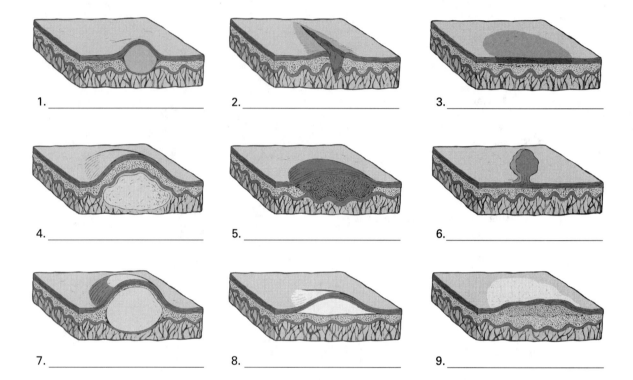

1. _____   2. _____   3. _____

4. _____   5. _____   6. _____

7. _____   8. _____   9. _____

Test 3D   Instructor's Answers: Common Skin Lesions

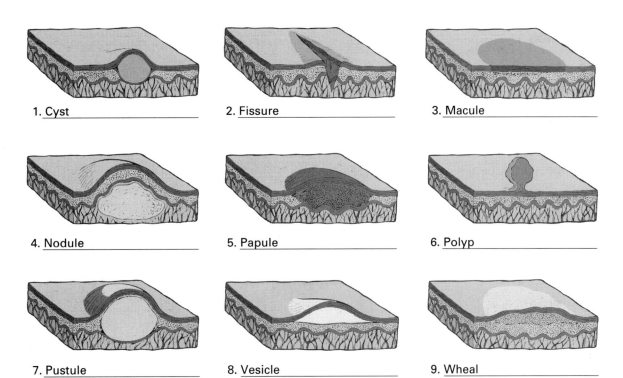

1. Cyst
2. Fissure
3. Macule
4. Nodule
5. Papule
6. Polyp
7. Pustule
8. Vesicle
9. Wheal

Name _____ Date _____ Errors _____

Test 3E Identifying Abbreviations

Write the definition of the abbreviation in the space provided.

	Abbreviation	Meaning
1.	BX	_____
2.	Derm	_____
3.	FS	_____
4.	H	_____
5.	I&D	_____
6.	ID	_____
7.	LE	_____
8.	SCLE	_____
9.	SG	_____
10.	STSG	_____
11.	SLE	_____
12.	STD	_____
13.	Subcu	_____
14.	Subq	_____
15.	UV	_____
16.	ung	_____

4

Musculoskeletal System

Learning Objectives

1. Identify the word roots and combining forms for this system.

   Note. You may wish to use Test 4A to assist in determining if the student has gained this knowledge.

	Word Root	**Meaning**
1.	ankyl/o	stiff joint
2.	arthr/o	joint
3.	brachi/o	arm
4.	burs/o	sac
5.	carp/o	wrist
6.	caud/o	tail
7.	cephal/o	head
8.	cervic/o	neck
9.	chrondr/o	cartilage
10.	cleid/o	clavicle
11.	condyl/o	condyle/bone protuberance
12.	cost/o	rib
13.	crani/o	head/skull
14.	dactyl/o	digit
15.	femor/o	femur/thigh bone
16.	fibul/o	fibula
17.	humer/o	humerus
18.	ili/o	ilium/part of hip bone
19.	ischi/o	hip
20.	lumb/o	loin/lower back
21.	maxill/o	upper jaw bone
22.	metacarp/o	metacarpus/bones of hand
23.	muscul/o	muscle
24.	myel/o	bone marrow/spinal cord
25.	my/o	muscle
26.	orth/o	straight

	Word Root	**Meaning**
27.	oste/o	bone
28.	patell/o	kneecap/patella
29.	ped/o	foot
30.	pelv/o	pelvis
31.	phalang/o	phalanges/bones of fingers and toes
32.	pub/o	pubis
33.	spondyl/o	vertebra/backbone
34.	stern/o	sternum/breastbone
35.	tars/o	foot
36.	ten/o	tendon
37.	tend/o	tendon
38.	tendin/o	tendon
39.	tens/o	stretch
40.	thorac/o	chest
41.	tibi/o	tibia/inner bone of lower leg
42.	vertebr/o	vertebra/backbone

2. Describe the organs of the musculoskeletal system and their function
   a. bones
   b. joints
   c. tendons
   d. muscles

   Note. You may wish to use Tests 4B to 4E to test students' knowledge of the major bones and muscles.

3. Build medical terms related to this system.

   Note. Have students use the word roots/combining forms and suffixes for the musculoskeletal system with the prefixes listed in chapter 1 to form terms. Students can check on the meaning of the terms they form by using a medical dictionary.

4. Identify and discuss related pathology to the musculoskeletal system.

   Note. You may wish to use Test 4F to test students' knowledge.

   Pathology Terms

   a. epidermoid cyst
   b. ganglion
   c. giant cell tumor
   d. hemangioma
   e. osteoblastoma
   f. osteochrondroma
   g. osteoid osteoma
   h. Ewing's sarcoma
   I. fibrosarcoma
   j. Paget's disease

5. Name and describe 10 major disorders of this system.

   Note. You may wish to use Test 4G to test students' knowledge.

Major Disorders

arthritis	bunion	bursitis
gout	kyphosis	lordosis
muscular dystrophy	myopathy	osteoarthritis
myasthenia gravis	osteomalacia	osteomyelitis
osteoporosis	polymyositis	rheumatoid arthritis
rickets	rigor mortis	scoliosis
spinal stenosis	talipes	varus
valgus	planus	equis
torsion	whiplash	
carpal tunnel syndrome		
ruptured intervertebral disk		
supernumerary bone		
systemic lupus erythematosis		

6. Identify 10 procedures that pertain to this system.

   Note. You may wish to use Test 4H to test students' understanding of procedures and diagnostic tests.

PROCEDURES

anterior cruciate ligament reconstruction (ACL)
amputation
arthrodesis
arthroplasty
arthroscopic surgery
arthrotomy
bone graft
bunionectomy
carpal tunnel release
cast
fasciectomy
laminectomy
menisectomy
reduction
spinal fusion
surgical fixation
total hip replacement

DIAGNOSTIC AND LABORATORY TESTS

arthrocentesis
arthrography
arthroscopy
bone scan
computerized axial tomography
electromyography
magnetic resonance imaging
myelography
muscle biopsy
photon absorptiometry

7. Interpret abbreviations used in the study of the musculoskeletal system.

   Note. You may wish to use Test 4I to test student's knowledge of abbreviations relating to the musculoskeletal system.

	Abbreviation	Meaning
1.	LAT	lateral
2.	ACL	anterior criciate ligament
3.	UE	upper extremity
4.	AP	anteroposterior
5.	TX	traction
6.	C1	first cervical vertebra
7.	TKR	total knee replacement
8.	Ca	calcium
9.	TKA	total knee arthroplasty
10.	CDH	congenital dislocation of the hip
11.	THR	total hip replacement
12.	CTS	carpal tunnel syndrome
13.	T2	second thoracic vertebra
14.	DTR	deep tendon reflex
15.	ROM	range of motion
16.	EMG	electromyography
17.	RIF	right iliac fossa
18.	FX	fracture
19.	RA	rheumatoid arthritis
20.	Ga	gallium
21.	ortho	orthopedics
22.	IM	intramuscular
23.	LUE	left upper extremity
24.	KB	knee bearing
25.	LOM	limitation of motion
26.	LE	lower extremity
27.	LLE	left lower extremity
28.	L1	first lumbar vertebra
29.	LIF	left iliac fossa

Pronunciation Guide: The Musculoskeletal System

Vocabulary Relating to the Musculoskeletal System

chiropodist (ki ROP oh dist)
chiropractic (ki ro PRAK tik)
orthopedics (or tho PE diks)
orthopedist (or tho PE dist)
orthotics (or THOT iks)
ossification (os eh fi KA shun)
orthotist (OR tho tist)
osteopathy (os te OP ath ee)
osteopath (OS te oh path)
prosthesis (pros THE sis)
podiatrist (po DIE ah trist)
physiatrist (fiz e AT rist)

Common Disorders of the Musculoskeletal System

arthritis (ar THRI tis)
bursitis (ber SI tis)
carpal tunnel syndrome (carpal tunnel syndrome)
gout (GOWT)
kyphosis (kye FOH sis)
lordosis (lor DOH sis)
muscular dystrophy (MUS ku lar/DIS tro fe)
myasthenia gravis (mi as THE ne ah/GRAV is)
myopathy (mi OP ah the)
osteoarthritis (os te o ar THRI tis)
osteomalacia (os te o mah LAY she ah)
osteomyelitis (os te o mi el I tis)
osteoporosis (os te o po ROE sis)
polymyositis (pol e mi oh SI tis)
rheumatoid arthritis (ROO ma toyd/ar THRI tis)
rickets (RIK ets)
rigor mortis (RIG ur/MOR tis)
ruptured intervertebral disk (ruptured/in ter VER te bral/disk)
scoliosis (sko le O sis)
spinal stenosis (spinal/ste NO sis)
supernumerary bone (soo per NU mer ar e/bone)
talipes (TAL ih pez)

Pathology Relating to the Musculoskeletal System

epidermoid (ep ih DER moyd)
ganglion (GANG le on)
hemangioma (he man je OH ma)
osteoblastoma (OS te oh blas to ma)
osteochondroma (os te oh kon DRO ma)
osteoid osteoma (OS te oyd/os te O ma)
Ewing's sarcoma (U ingz/sar CO ma)
fibrosarcoma (fi bro sar KO ma)
Paget's disease (PAJ etz/ disease)

Procedures Relating to the Musculoskeletal System

anterior cruciate ligament (anterior/KROO she ate/ligament)
arthrodesis (ar thro DE sis)
arthroplasty (AR thro plas tee)
arthroscopic (ar thro SKOP ic)
arthrotomy (ar THROT oh me)
bunionectomy (bun yun EK to me)
carpal tunnel release (KAR pal/tunnel/release)
fasciectomy (fas e EK to me)
laminectomy (lam eh NEK to me)
menisectomy (men eh SEK to me)

Diagnostic and Laboratory Tests of the Musculoskeletal System

arthrocentesis (ar thro sen TEE sis)
arthrography (ar THROG rah fe)
arthroscopy (ar THROS ko pe)
computerized axial tomography (computerized/axial/to MOG rah fe)
electromyography (e lek tro mi OG rah fe)
magnetic resonance imaging (magnetic resonance imaging)
myelography (mi e LOG rah fe)
photon absorptiometry (FO ton/ab zorp she OM e tre)

Name _____ Date _____ Errors _____

Test 4A Defining Word Roots/Combining Form

Define the word root/combining form in the space provided.

	Word Root	Meaning
1.	ankyl/o	
2.	arthr/o	
3.	brachi/o	
4.	burs/o	
5.	carp/o	
6.	caud/o	
7.	cephal/o	
8.	cervic/o	
9.	chrondr/o	
10.	cleid/o	
11.	condyl/o	
12.	cost/o	
13.	crani/o	
14.	dactyl/o	
15.	femor/o	
16.	fibul/o	
17.	humer/o	
18.	ili/o	
19.	ischi/o	
20.	lumb/o	
21.	maxill/o	
22.	metacarp/o	
23.	muscul/o	
24.	myel/o	
25.	my/o	
26.	orth/o	
27.	oste/o	
28.	patell/o	

	Word Root	Meaning
29.	ped/o	
30.	pelv/o	
31.	phalang/o	
32.	pub/o	
33.	spondyl/o	
34.	stern/o	
35.	tars/o	
36.	ten/o	
37.	tend/o	
38.	tendin/o	
39.	tens/o	
40.	thorac/o	
41.	tibi/o	
42.	vertebr/o	

Name _____ Date _____ Errors _____

Test 4B Identifying Bones

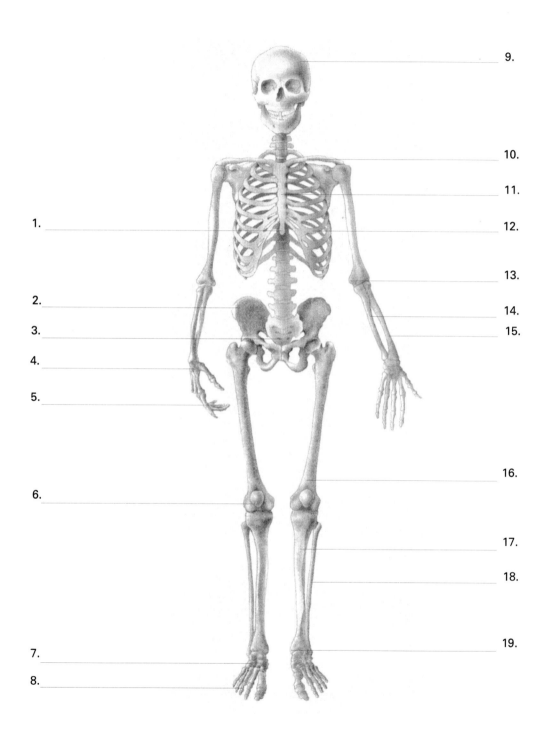

1. _____
2. _____
3. _____
4. _____
5. _____
6. _____
7. _____
8. _____

9. _____
10. _____
11. _____
12. _____
13. _____
14. _____
15. _____
16. _____
17. _____
18. _____
19. _____

Chapter 4 Musculoskeletal System **53**

Name _____ Date _____ Errors _____

Test 4B Instructor's Answers: Identifying Bones

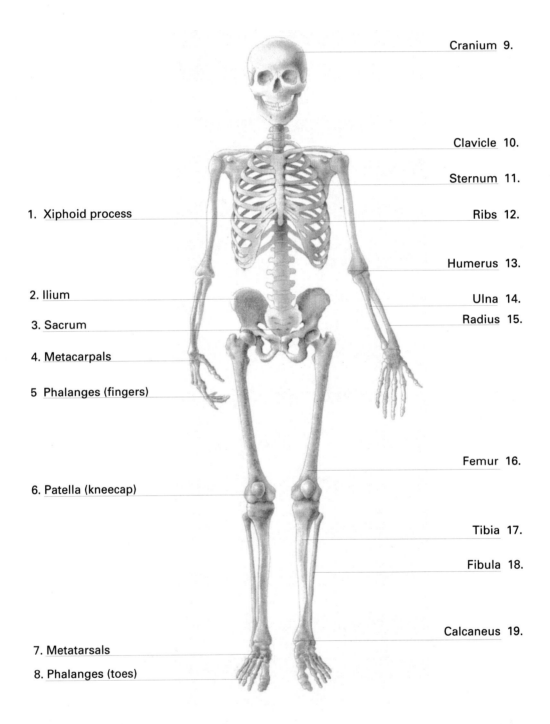

1. Xiphoid process
2. Ilium
3. Sacrum
4. Metacarpals
5. Phalanges (fingers)
6. Patella (kneecap)
7. Metatarsals
8. Phalanges (toes)

9. Cranium
10. Clavicle
11. Sternum
12. Ribs
13. Humerus
14. Ulna
15. Radius
16. Femur
17. Tibia
18. Fibula
19. Calcaneus

Name _____ Date _____ Errors _____

Test 4C   Identifying Cranial and Facial Bones

1. _____
2. _____
3. _____
4. _____
5. _____
6. _____
7. _____
8. _____
9. _____

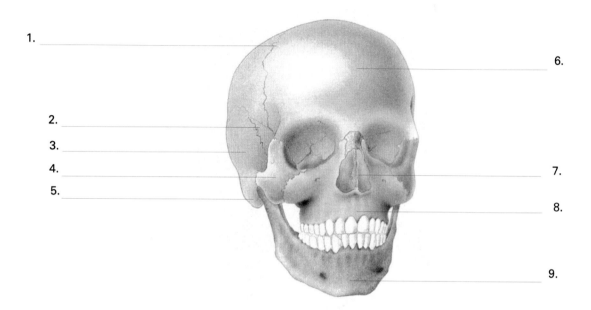

Chapter 4   Musculoskeletal System   **55**

Name _____ Date _____ Errors _____

Test 4C   Instructor's Answers: Identifying Cranial and Facial Bones

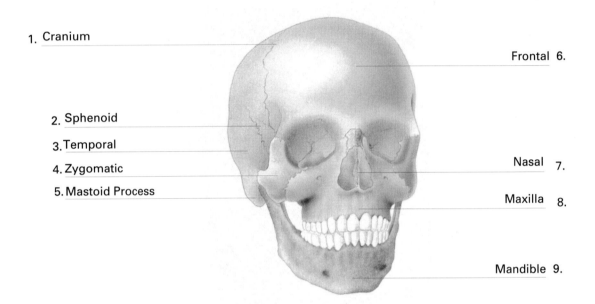

1. Cranium
2. Sphenoid
3. Temporal
4. Zygomatic
5. Mastoid Process
6. Frontal
7. Nasal
8. Maxilla
9. Mandible

Name _____ **Date** _____ **Errors** _____

Test 4D   Identifying Bones of the Vertebral Column

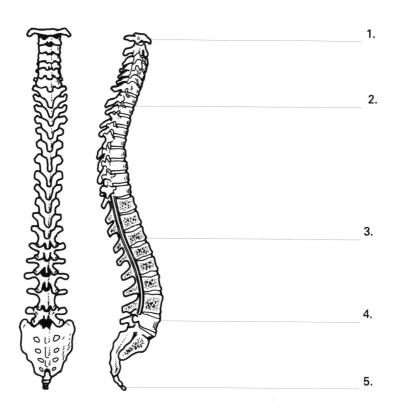

1. _____

2. _____

3. _____

4. _____

5. _____

Chapter 4   Musculoskeletal System   **57**

Name _____ Date _____ Errors _____

Test 4D   Instructor's Answers: Identifying Bones of the Vertebral Column

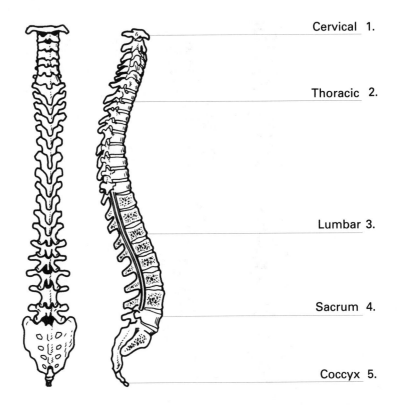

1. Cervical
2. Thoracic
3. Lumbar
4. Sacrum
5. Coccyx

Name _____ Date _____ Errors _____

Test 4E Identifying Major Muscles

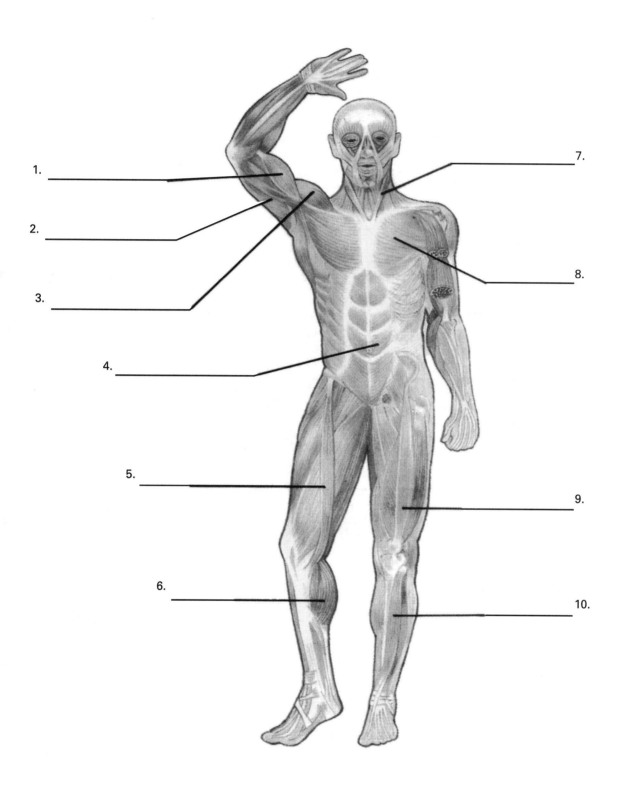

Chapter 4   Musculoskeletal System   **59**

Name _____ Date _____ Errors _____

Test 4E   Instructor's Answers: Identifying Major Muscles

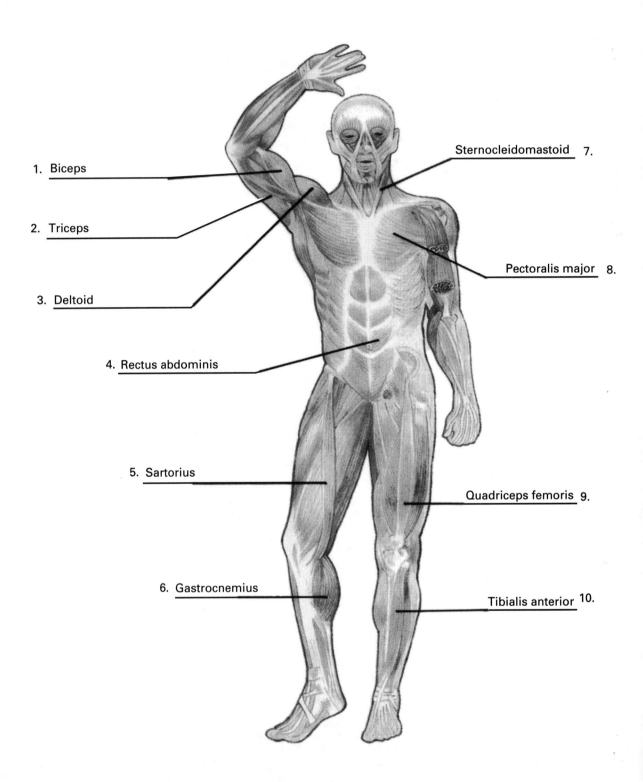

1. Biceps
2. Triceps
3. Deltoid
4. Rectus abdominis
5. Sartorius
6. Gastrocnemius
7. Sternocleidomastoid
8. Pectoralis major
9. Quadriceps femoris
10. Tibialis anterior

Name _____ Date _____ Errors _____

Test 4F Pathology of the Musculoskeletal System

Write the definition in the space provided.

Pathology Terms

a. epidermoid cyst _____

b. ganglion _____

c. giant cell tumor _____

d. hemangioma _____

e. osteoblastoma _____

f. osteochondroma _____

g. osteoid osteoma _____

h. Ewing's sarcoma _____

i. fibrosarcoma _____

j. Paget's disease _____

Name _____ Date _____ Errors _____

Test 4G   Major Disorders of the Musculoskeletal System

Define the medical condition in the space provided.

Major Disorders

1. arthritis _____
2. bunion _____
3. bursitis _____
4. gout _____
5. kyphosis _____
6. lordosis _____
7. muscular dystrophy _____
8. myopathy _____
9. osteoarthritis _____
10. myasthenia gravis _____
11. osteomalacia _____
12. osteomyelitis _____
13. osteoporosis _____
14. polymyositis _____
15. rheumatoid arthritis _____
16. rickets _____
17. rigor mortis _____
18. scoliosis _____
19. spinal stenosis _____
20. talipes _____
21. varus _____
22. valgus _____
23. planus _____
24. equis _____
25. torsion _____
26. whiplash _____
27. carpal tunnel syndrome _____
28. ruptured intervertebral disk _____
29. supernumerary bone _____
30. systemic lupus erythematosis _____

Name _____ Date _____ Errors _____

Test 4H   Procedures and Diagnostic Tests of the Musculoskeletal System

Define the following terms in the space provided:

Procedures

1. anterior cruciate ligament reconstruction (ACL) _____
2. amputation _____
3. arthrodesis _____
4. arthroplasty _____
5. arthroscopic surgery _____
6. arthrotomy _____
7. bone graft _____
8. bunionectomy _____
9. carpal tunnel release _____
10. cast _____
11. fasciectomy _____
12. laminectomy _____
13. menisectomy _____
14. reduction _____
15. spinal fusion _____
16. surgical fixation _____
17. total hip replacement _____

Diagnostic and Laboratory Tests

1. arthrocentesis _____
2. arthrography _____
3. arthroscopy _____
4. bone scan _____
5. computerized axial tomography _____
6. electromyography _____
7. magnetic resonance imaging _____
8. myelography _____
9. muscle biopsy _____
10. photon absorptiometry _____

Name _____ Date _____ Errors _____

Test 4I Identifying Abbreviations

Write the definition of the abbreviation in the space provided.

	Abbreviation	Definition
1.	LAT	
2.	ACL	
3.	UE	
4.	AP	
5.	TX	
6.	C1	
7.	TKR	
8.	Ca	
9.	TKA	
10.	CDH	
11.	THR	
12.	CTS	
13.	T2	
14.	DTR	
15.	ROM	
16.	EMG	
17.	RIF	
18.	FX	
19.	RA	
20.	Ga	
21.	ortho	
22.	IM	
23.	LUE	
24.	KB	
25.	LOM	
26.	LE	
27.	LLE	
28.	L1	
29.	LIF	

5

Endocrine System

Learning Objectives

1. Identify the word roots and combining forms relating to the endocrine system.

   Note. You may wish to use Test 5A to assist in determining if students have gained this knowledge.

	Word Root	Meaning
1.	cortic/o	cortex, outer layer
2.	insulin/o	insulin
3.	natr/o	sodium
4.	acr/o	enlarged
5.	calc/o	calcium
6.	kal/i	potassium
7.	thym/o	thymus
8.	aden/o	gland
9.	crin/o	secrete
10.	thyr/o	thyroid
11.	adren/o	adrenal
12.	dips/o	thirst
13.	gonad/o	sex gland
14.	pancreat/o	pancreas
15.	thyroid/o	thyroid
16.	adrenal/o	adrenal
17.	gluc/o	sugar
18.	parathyroid/o	parathyroid
19.	ster/o	steroid
20.	glyc/o	sugar
21.	pituitar/o	pituitary
22.	toxic/o	toxic, poison
23.	hormon/o	hormone
24.	myx/o	mucus

2. Describe the organs of the endocrine system and their function.

   Note. You may wish to use Test 5B to evaluate students' knowledge.

3. Build terms related to the endocrine system.

   Note. You may wish to use Test 5C to have students build terms using word roots/combining form related to the endocrine system with previously learned suffixes and prefixes from chapter 1.

4. Identify and discuss pathology related to the endocrine system.

   Note. You may wish to test students on the following terms by using Test 5D.

acidosis	acromegaly	adenoma
Addison's disease	cretinism	Cushing's syndrome
diabetes insipidus	diabetes mellitus	diabetic retinopathy
dwarfism	gigantism	goiter
Graves's disease	hyperthyroidism	Hashimoto's disease
hypothyroidism	ketosis	ketoacidosis
myasthenia gravis	myxedema	thyrotoxicosis
von Recklinghausen's disease		

5. Name and describe the 10 major disorders that relate to the endocrine system.

   Note. You may wish to test the student on the following terms by using Test 5D.

   hirsutism
   hypercalcemia
   hyperglycemia
   hyperkalemia
   obesity

6. Identify 10 procedures that pertain to the endocrine system.

   Note. You may wish to test students on the following terms by using Test 5E.

   adrenalectomy
   parathyroidectomy
   thymectomy
   thyroidectomy
   thyroparathyroidectomy
   basal metabolic rate (BMR)
   blood serum tests
   fasting blood sugar
   computerized tomography scan (CT)
   serum glucose tests
   thyroid echogram
   thyroid scan
   total calcium test
   two-hour postprandial glucose tolerance test
   thyroid function tests
   glucose tolerance test (GTT)
   protein-bound iodine test (PBI)
   radioactive iodine uptake test (RAIU)
   radioimmunoassay (RIA)

7. Interpret abbreviations used in the study of the endocrine system.

   Note. You may wish to use Test 5F to test students' knowledge of abbreviations relating to the endocrine system.

	Abbreviation	**Meaning**
1.	FBS	fasting blood sugar
2.	RAIU	radioactive iodine uptake
3.	ACTH	adrenocorticotropic hormone
4.	FSH	follicle-stimulating hormone
5.	RAI	radioactive iodine
6.	ADH	antidiuretic hormone
7.	GH	growth hormone
8.	T3	triiodothyronine
9.	BMR	basal metabolic rate
10.	GTT	glucose tolerance test
11.	T4	thyroxine
12.	DI	diabetes insipidus
13.	HDL	high-density lipoproteins
14.	T7	free thyroxine index
15.	DM	diabetes mellitus
16.	HGH	human growth hormone
17.	TFT	thyroid function test
18.	PBI	protein bound iodine
19.	IDDM	insulin-dependent diabetes mellitus
20.	TSH	thyroid-stimulating hormone
21.	PGH	pituitary growth hormone
22.	K	potassium
23.	VLDL	very low-density lipoproteins
24.	Na	sodium
25.	XX	female sex chromosome
26.	PTH	parathyroid hormone
27.	NIDDM	non-insulin-dependent diabetes
28.	XY	male sex chromosomes
29.	NPH	neutral protamine Hagedorn (insulin)
30.	MSH	melanocyte-stimulating hormone

Pronunciation Guide: The Endocrine System

Vocabulary Relating to the Endocrine System

endocrinologist (en do kri NOL oh jist)
endocrinology (en do kri NOL oh je)
exophthalmos (ex of THAL mos)
glycosuria (gli ko SU re ah)
metabolism (me TAB oh lizm)
oral hypoglycemic agent (oral/hi po gli SEE mik/agent)
polydipsia (pol ee DIP se ah)
polyuria (pol ee UR ree ah)
syndrome (SIN drome)

Common Disorders of the Endocrine System

hirsutism (her SOOT izm)
hypercalcemia (hi per kal SE me ah)
hypergylcemia (hi per gli SEE me ah)
hyperkalemia (hi per ka LE me ah)
obesity (o BE si te)

Pathology Relating to the Endocrine System

acidosis (as eh DO sis)
acromegaly (ak ro MEG ah le)
adenoma (ad ee NO ma)
Addison's disease (Addison's disease)
cretinism (KRE tin izm)
Cushing's syndrome (Cushing's syndrome)
diabetes insipidus (di ah BE tez/in SIP eh diz)
diabetes mellitus (di ah BE tez/me LI tiz)
diabetic retinopathy (di ah BE tik/ret eh NOP ah the)
gigantism (ji GAN tizm)
goiter (GOY tur)
Hashimoto's disease (Hashimoto's disease)
hyperthyroidism (hi pur THI roi dizm)
hypothyroidism (hi po THI royd izm)
ketosis (ke TO sis)
ketoacidosis (ke to ah si DO sis)
myasthenia gravis (mi as THE ne ah/GRA vis)
myxedema (mik se DE ma)
thyrotoxicosis (thi ro tok si KO sis)
von Recklinghausen's disease (von Recklinghausen's disease)

Procedures Relating to the Endocrine System

adrenalectomy (ad re nal EK to me)
parathyroidectomy (par ah thi roi DEK to me)
thymectomy (thi MEK to me)
thyroidectomy (thi roi DEK to me)
thyroparathyroidectomy (thr ro par ah thi royd EK to me)

Diagnostic and Laboratory Tests of the Endocrine System

computerized tomography (computerized/ toe MOG ra fe)
radioimmunoassay (ra de o im u nò AS a)
thyroid echogram (thyroid/ EK oh gram)
two-hour postprandial glucose tolerance test (two-hour/post PRAN de al/glucose/ tolerance /test)

Name _____ Date _____ Errors _____

Test 5A   Identifying Word Roots with Combining Form

Write the definition of the word root in the space provided.

	Word Root	Meaning
1.	cortic/o	
2.	insulin/o	
3.	natr/o	
4.	acr/o	
5.	calc/o	
6.	kal/i	
7.	thym/o	
8.	aden/o	
9.	crin/o	
10.	thyr/o	
11.	adren/o	
12.	dips/o	
13.	gonad/o	
14.	pancreat/o	
15.	thyroid/o	
16.	adrenal/o	
17.	gluc/o	
18.	parathyroid/o	
19.	ster/o	
20.	glyc/o	
21.	pituitar/o	
22.	toxic/o	
23.	hormon/o	
24.	myx/o	

Name _____ Date _____ Errors _____

Test 5B   Identifying Organs of the Endocrine System

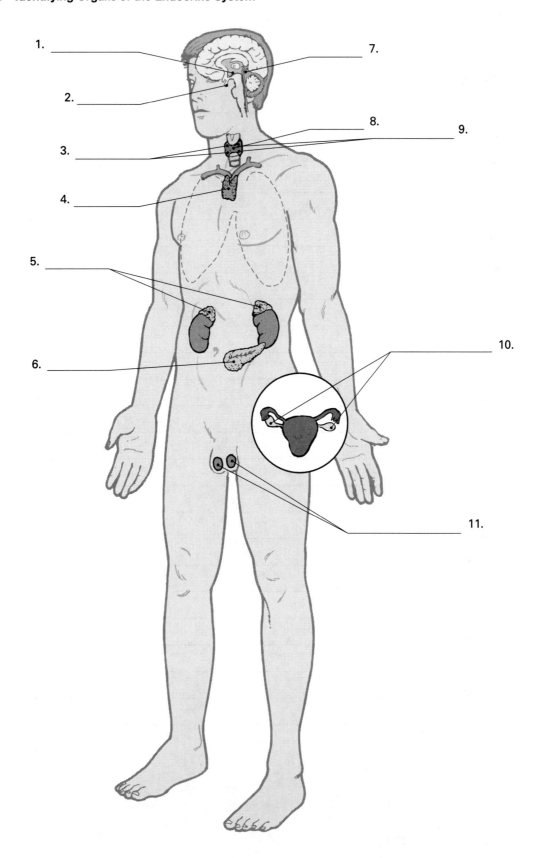

72   INSTRUCTOR'S GUIDE   MEDICAL TERMINOLOGY

Name _____ Date _____ Errors _____

Test 5B Instructor's Answers: Identifying Organs of the Endocrine System

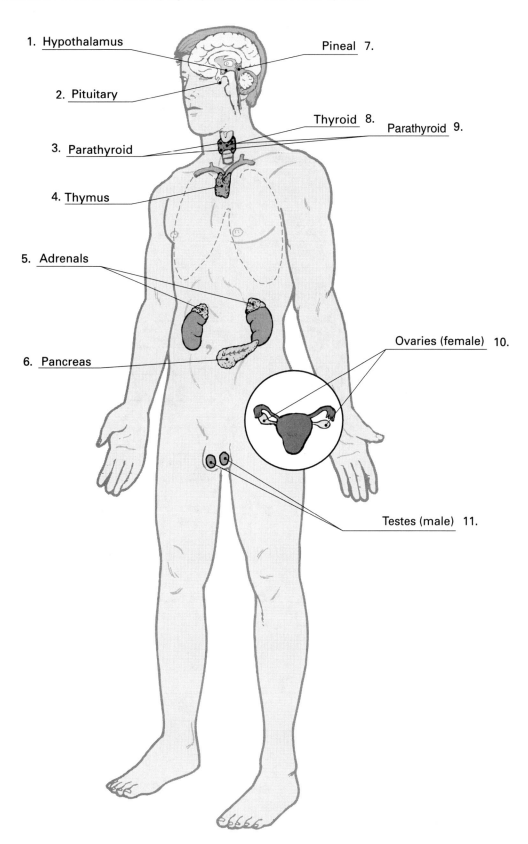

Chapter 5 Endocrine System   73

Name _____ Date _____ Errors _____

Test 5C Building Terms Related to the Endocrine System

Using prefixes and/or suffixes, build medical terms using the following word roots/combining forms:

	Word Root	New Term
1.	cortic/o	_____
2.	insulin/o	_____
3.	natr/o	_____
4.	acr/o	_____
5.	calc/o	_____
6.	kal/i	_____
7.	thym/o	_____
8.	aden/o	_____
9.	crin/o	_____
10.	thyr/o	_____
11.	adren/o	_____
12.	dips/o	_____
13.	gonad/o	_____
14.	pancreat/o	_____
15.	thyroid/o	_____
16.	adrenal/o	_____
17.	gluc/o	_____
18.	parathyroid/o	_____
19.	ster/o	_____
20.	glyc/o	_____
21.	pituitar/o	_____
22.	toxic/o	_____
23.	hormon/o	_____
24.	myx/o	_____

Name _____ Date _____ Errors _____

Test 5D Define the following terms in the space provided:

1. acidosis _____
   _____

2. acromegaly _____
   _____

3. adenoma _____
   _____

4. Addison's disease _____
   _____

5. cretinism _____
   _____

6. Cushing's syndrome _____
   _____

7. diabetes insipidus _____
   _____

8. diabetes mellitus _____
   _____

9. diabetic retinopathy _____
   _____

10. dwarfism _____
    _____

11. gigantism_____
    _____

12. goiter _____
    _____

13. Graves's disease _____
    _____

14. hyperthyroidism_____
    _____

15. Hashimoto's disease _____
    _____

16. hypothyroidism _____
    _____

17. ketosis _____
    _____

18. ketoacidosis _____
    _____

19. myasthenia gravis _____
    _____

20. myxedema _____
    _____

21. thyrotoxicosis _____
    _____

22. von Recklinghausen's disease _____
    _____

23. hirsutism _____
    _____

24. hypercalcemia _____
    _____

25. hyperglycemia _____
    _____

26. hyperkalemia _____
    _____

27. obesity _____
    _____

Name _____ Date _____ Errors _____

Test 5E   Procedures, Diagnostic and Laboratory Tests of the Endocrine System

Write a definition of the term in the space provided.

1. adrenalectomy _____

2. parathyroidectomy _____

3. thymectomy _____

4. thyroidectomy _____

5. thyroparathyroidectomy _____

6. basal metabolic rate (BMR) _____

7. blood serum tests _____

8. fasting blood sugar _____

9. computerized tomography scan (CT) _____

10. serum glucose tests _____

11. thyroid echogram _____

12. thyroid scan _____

13. total calcium test _____

14. two-hour postprandial glucose tolerance test _____

Chapter 5   Endocrine System

15. thyroid function tests _____

16. glucose tolerance test (GTT) _____

17. protein-bound iodine test (PBI) _____

18. radioactive iodine uptake test (RAIU) _____

19. radioimmunoassay (RIA) _____

Name _____ Date _____ Errors _____

Test 5F   Identifying Abbreviations

Write the definition of the abbreviation in the space provided.

	Abbreviation	Definition
1.	FBS	
2.	RAIU	
3.	ACTH	
4.	FSH	
5.	RAI	
6.	ADH	
7.	GH	
8.	T3	
9.	BMR	
10.	GTT	
11.	T4	
12.	DI	
13.	HDL	
14.	T7	
15.	DM	
16.	HGH	
17.	TFT	
18.	PBI	
19.	IDDM	
20.	TSH	
21.	PGH	
22.	K	
23.	VLDL	
24.	Na	
25.	XX	
26.	PTH	
27.	NIDDM	
28.	XY	
29.	NPH	
30.	MSH	

6

Cardiovascular System

Learning Objectives

1. Identify the word roots and combining forms relating to the cardiovascular system.

   Note. You may wish to use Test 6A to assist in determining if the student has gained this knowledge.

	Word Root	**Meaning**
1.	venul/o	venule
2.	ventricul/o	ventricle
3.	angi/o	blood vessel
4.	ven/o	vein
5.	arteri/o	artery
6.	vas/o	vessel
7.	ather/o	fatty substance/plaque
8.	valv/o	valve
9.	atri/o	atrium
10.	thromb/o	clot
11.	cardi/o	heart
12.	valvul/o	valve
13.	cor/o	heart
14.	steth/o	chest
15.	embol/o	embolus
16.	sphygm/o	pulse
17.	coron/o	heart
18.	phleb/o	vein
19.	hemangi/o	blood vessel
20.	oxy/o	oxygen
21.	my/o	muscle

2. Describe the organs of the cardiovascular system and their function.

   Note. You may wish to use Tests 6B and 6C to evaluate students' knowledge.

3. Build terms related to this system.

   Note. You may wish to use Test 6D to have students build terms using word roots/combining form related to the endocrine system with previously learned suffixes and prefixes from chapter 1.

4. Identify and discuss pathology related to the cardiovascular system.

   Note. You may wish to test students on the following terms related to pathology. This list can also be used to test spelling and dictation skills.

angiocarditis	angina pectoris	angioma
angiospasm	aortic aneurysm	aortic insufficiency
aortic stenosis	arrhythmia	arterial embolism
arteriosclerosis	atherosclerosis	bradycardia
bruit	coarctation	coronary ischemia
coronary thrombosis	embolus	endocarditis
fibrillation	hypotension	hypertension
infarct	ischemia	mitral stenosis
murmur	pericarditis	phlebitis
shunt	thrombophlebitis	varicose veins

   atrioventricular defect
   congenital heart disease
   congestive heart failure
   congenital septal defect
   hypertensive heart disease
   myocardial infarction
   patent ductus arteriosus
   Raynaud's phenomenon
   rheumatic heart disease
   tetralogy of Fallot

5. Identify 10 procedures that pertain to the cardiovascular system.

   Note. You may wish to test students on the following terms related to procedures. This list can also be used to test spelling and dictation skills.

aneurysmectomy	angioplasty	artery graft
artificial pacemaker	blood pressure	cardiolysis
cardiorrhaphy	cardiotomy	cardioversion
commissurotomy	embolectomy	pericardectomy
phleborrhaphy	phlebotomy	pulse
thrombectomy	valve replacement	venipuncture
venotomy	open-heart surgery	

   coarctation of the aorta
   coronary artery bypass surgery
   heart transplantation
   mitral commissurotomy
   percutaneous transluminal angioplasty
   percutaneous balloon valvuloplasty

6. Interpret abbreviations used in the study of this system.

   Note. You may wish to use Test 6E to evaluate students' knowledge of abbreviations relating to the cardiovascular system.

	Abbreviation	Meaning
1.	ADL	activities of daily living
2.	AI	aortic insufficiency
3.	AF	atrial fibrillation
4.	AMI	acute myocardial infarction
5.	APB	atrial premature beat
6.	AS	aortic stenosis, arteriosclerosis
7.	ASCVD	arteriosclerotic cardiovascular disease
8.	ASD	atrial septal defect
9.	ASHD	arteriosclerotic heart disease
10.	AV, A-V	atrioventricular
11.	BBB	bundle branch block
12.	BP	blood pressure
13.	CABG	coronary artery bypass graft
14.	CAD	coronary artery disease
15.	cath	catheterization
16.	CCU	coronary care unit
17.	CHD	congestive heart disease
18.	CHF	congestive heart failure
19.	CIC	coronary intensive care
20.	CPR	cardiopulmonary resuscitation
21.	DVT	deep vein thrombosis
22.	ECG, EKG	electrocardiogram
23.	HDL	high-density lipoproteins
24.	HTN	hypertension
25.	IVCD	intraventricular conduction delay
26.	JVP	jugular venous pulse
27.	LDL	low-density lipoproteins
28.	LVAD	left ventricular assist device
29.	MI	myocardial infarction, mitral insufficiency
30.	mm Hg	millimeters of mercury
31.	MR	mitral regurgitation
32.	MS	mitral stenosis
33.	MVP	mitral valve prolapse
34.	NSR	normal sinus rhythm
35.	P	pulse
36.	PAP	pulmonary artery pressure
37.	PAT	paroxysmal atrial tachycardia
38.	PTCA	percutaneous transluminal coronary angioplasty
39.	PVC	premature ventricular contraction
40.	SA, S-A	sinoatrial
41.	S1	first heart sound
42.	S2	second heart sound
43.	SBE	subacute bacterial endocarditis
44.	SGOT	serum glutamic oxaloacetic transaminase
45.	SK	streptokinase
46.	SVT	supraventricular tachycardia
47.	VPB	ventricular premature beat
48.	VSD	ventricular septal defect
49.	WPW	Wolff-Parkinson-White syndrome

PRONUNCIATION GUIDE: THE CARDIOVASCULAR SYSTEM

Vocabulary Relating to the Cardiovascular System

cardiomyopathy (kar de oh my OP ah the)
cardioverter (KAR de oh ver tor)
coronary (KOR o na re)
cyanosis (si ah NO sis)

Pathology Relating to the Cardiovascular System

angiocarditis (an je oh kar DI tis)
angina pectoris (an JI nah/PEK tor is)
angioma (an je O ma)
angiospasm (AN je o spazm)
aortic aneurysm (a OR tik/AN yu rizm)
aortic stenosis (a OR tik/ste NO sis)
arrhythmia (ah RITH me ah)
arterial embolism (ar TE re al/EM bo lizm)
arteriosclerosis (ar te re oh SKLE ro sis)
arteriosclerotic heart disease (ar te re o skle ROT ik/heart/disease)
atherosclerosis (ath ero SKLER oh sis)
atrioventricular defect (a tre o ven TRIK u lar/defect)
bradycardia (brad ee KAR de ah)
bruit (BROOT)
coarctation (ko ark TA shun)
coronary ischemia (KOR o na re/is KE me ah)
coronary thrombosis (KOR o na re/throm BO sis)
embolus (EM bo lus)
endocarditis (en do kar DI tis)
fibrillation (fi bril A shun)
hypertensive heart disease (hi per TEN sive/heart /disease)
hypotension (hi po TEN shun)
infarct (in FARCT)
ischemia (is KE me ah)
mitral stenosis (MI tral/ste NO sis)
mitral valve prolapse (mitral valve prolapse)
myocardial infarction (mi oh KAR de al/in FARC shun)
murmur (MUR mur)
patent ductus arteriosus (PA tent/DUK tus/ar te re OH sus)
pericarditis (per ee kar DI tis)
phlebitis(fle BI tis)
Raynaud's phenomenon (ra NOZ /FI nam ah nan)
rheumatic heart disease (roo MAT ik/heart/disease)

tetralogy of Fallot (te TRAL oh je/of/fal OH)
thrombophlebitis (throm bo fle BI tis)
varicose veins (VAR ee kos/veins)

Procedures Relating to the Cardiovascular System

aneurysmectomy (an u riz MEK to me)
angioplasty (AN je oh plas te)
cardiolysis (kar de OL i sis)
cardiotomy (kar de OT o me)
cardioversion (KAR de oh ver shun)
coarctation of the aorta (ko ark TA shun/of/the/aorta)
commissurotomy (kom eh shur OT oh me)
embolectomy (em bo LEK to me)
mitral commissurotomy (MI tral/kom eh shur OT oh me)
pericardiectomy (per ee kar de EK to me)
percutaneous transluminal angioplasty (per ku TA ne us/trans LOO mi nal/AN je oh plas te)
percutaneous balloon valvuloplasty (per ku TA ne us/balloon/VAL vu lo plas te)
phleborrhaphy (fleb OR a fe)
phlebotomy (fle BOT oh me)
thrombectomy (throm BEK to me)
venipuncture (VEN eh punk tur)
venotomy (ve NOT to me)

Diagnostic and Laboratory Tests of the Cardiovascular System

angiocardiography (an je oh kar de OG rah fe)
angiography (an je OG rah fe)
arterial (ar TE re al)
arteriography (ar te re OG rah fe)
cardiac catheterization (KAR de ak/kath e ter ih ZA shun)
cardiac enzymes (caridac/EN zimes)
cardiac magnetic resonance imaging (cardiac magnetic resonance imaging)
Doppler ultrasonography (DOP lur/ul tra son OG ra fe)
echocardiogram (ek o KAR de o gram)
electrolytes (e LEK tro lits)
electrocardiogram (e lek tro KAR de oh gram)
Holter monitor (Holter monitor)
lipoproteins (lip oh PRO teins)
prothrombin time (pro THROM bin/time)
venography (ve NOG ra fe)

Name _____ Date _____ Errors _____

Test 6A   Identifying Word Roots and Combining Forms

Write the meaning of the word root/combining form in the space provided.

	Word Root	**Meaning**
1.	venul/o	
2.	ventricul/o	
3.	angi/o	
4.	ven/o	
5.	arteri/o	
6.	vas/o	
7.	ather/o	
8.	valv/o	
9.	atri/o	
10.	thromb/o	
11.	cardi/o	
12.	valvul/o	
13.	cor/o	
14.	steth/o	
15.	embol/o	
16.	sphygm/o	
17.	coron/o	
18.	phleb/o	
19.	hemangi/o	
20.	oxy/o	
21.	my/o	

Name _____ Date _____ Errors _____

Test 6 Identifying Circulatory System Major Arteries and Veins

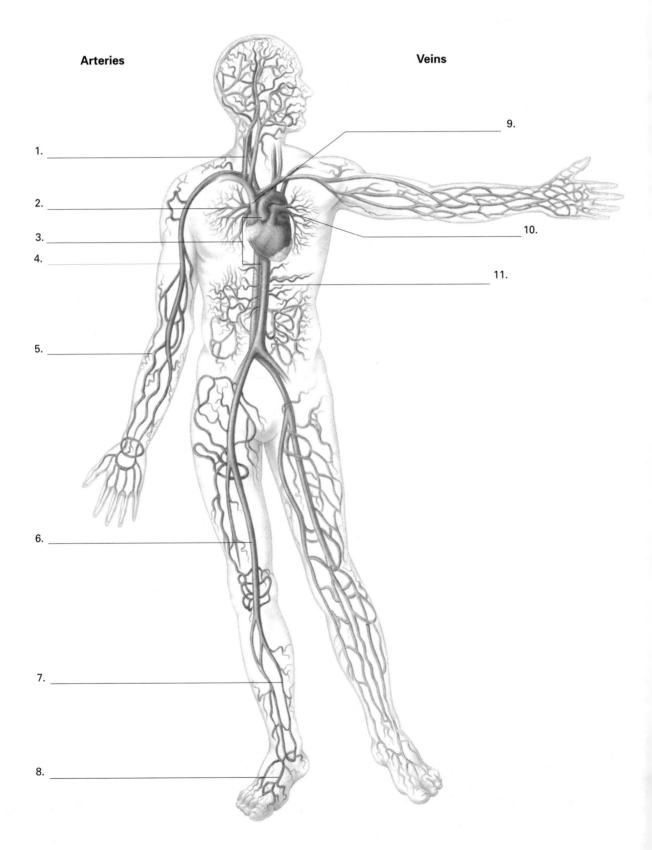

88 INSTRUCTOR'S GUIDE MEDICAL TERMINOLOGY

Name _____ Date _____ Errors _____

Test 6B   Instructor's Answers: Circulatory System Major Arteries are Veins

Arteries

Veins

1. Right carotid artery
2. Pulmonary artery
3. Aorta
4. Brachial artery
5. Radial artery
6. Femoral artery
7. Posterior tibial
8. Dorsalis pedis

9. Superior vena cava
10. Pulmonary vein
11. Inferior vena cava

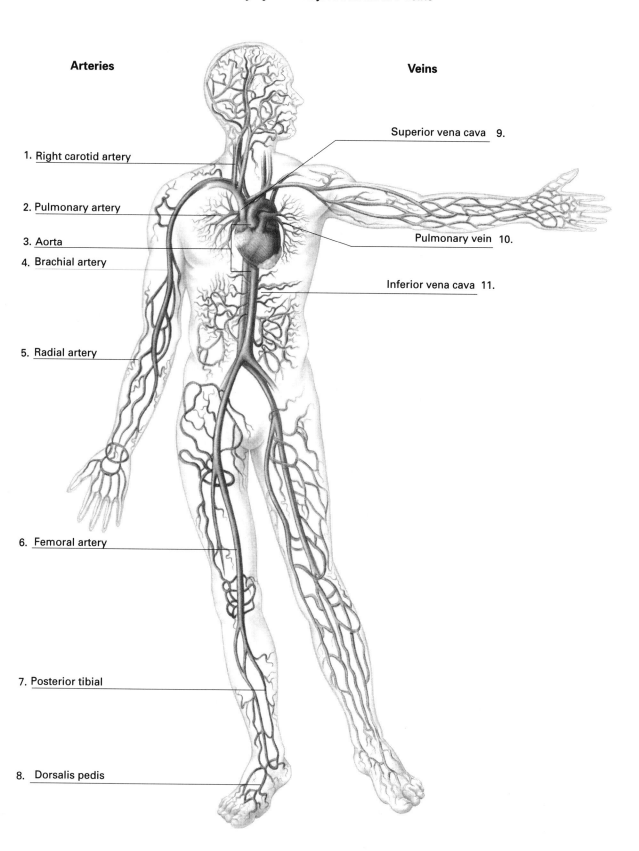

Chapter 6   Cardiovascular System   **89**

Name _____ Date _____ Errors _____

Test 6C Identifying Heart Chambers, Aorta, and Superior Vena Cava

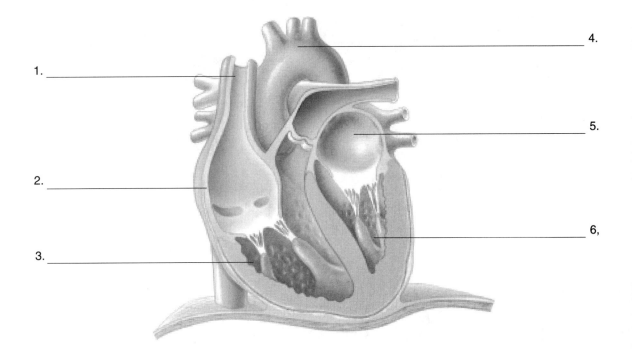

1. _____
2. _____
3. _____
4. _____
5. _____
6. _____

Name _____ Date _____ Errors _____

Test 6C Instructor's Answers: Heart Chambers, Aorta, and Superior Vena Cava

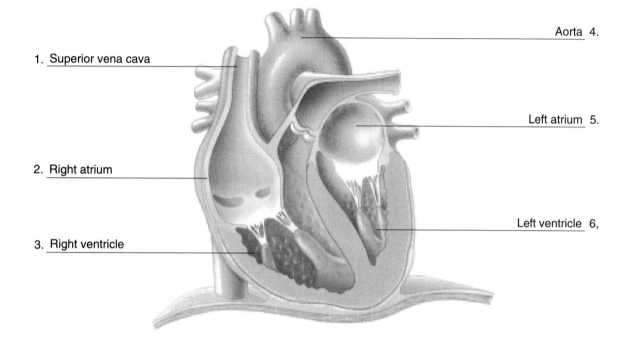

1. Superior vena cava
2. Right atrium
3. Right ventricle
4. Aorta
5. Left atrium
6. Left ventricle

Name _____ Date _____ Errors _____

Test 6D Building Terms Related to the Cardiovascular System

Using prefixes and/or suffixes, build medical terms using the following word roots/combining forms:

	Word Root	New Term
1.	venul/o	
2.	ventricul/o	
3.	angi/o	
4.	ven/o	
5.	arteri/o	
6.	vas/o	
7.	ather/o	
8.	valv/o	
9.	atri/o	
10.	thromb/o	
11.	cardi/o	
12.	valvul/o	
13.	cor/o	
14.	steth/o	
15.	embol/o	
16.	sphygm/o	
17.	coron/o	
18.	phleb/o	
19.	hemangi/o	
20.	oxy/o	
21.	my/o	

Name _____ Date _____ Errors _____

Test 6E Identifying Abbreviations

Write the definition of the abbreviation in the space provided.

	Abbreviation	Definition
1.	ADL	_____
2.	AI	_____
3.	AF	_____
4.	AMI	_____
5.	APB	_____
6.	AS	_____
7.	ASCVD	_____
8.	ASD	_____
9.	ASHD	_____
10.	AV, A-V	_____
11.	BBB	_____
12.	BP	_____
13.	CABG	_____
14.	CAD	_____
15.	cath	_____
16.	CCU	_____
17.	CHD	_____
18.	CHF	_____
19.	CIC	_____
20.	CPR	_____
21.	DVT	_____
22.	ECG, EKG	_____
23.	HDL	_____
24.	HTN	_____
25.	IVCD	_____
26.	JVP	_____
27.	LDL	_____
28.	LVAD	_____

	Abbreviation	Definition
29.	MI	_____
30.	mm Hg	_____
31.	MR	_____
32.	MS	_____
33.	MVP	_____
34.	NSR	_____
35.	P	_____
36.	PAP	_____
37.	PAT	_____
38.	PTCA	_____
39.	PVC	_____
40.	SA, S-A	_____
41.	S1	_____
42.	S2	_____
43.	SBE	_____
44.	SGOT	_____
45.	SK	_____
46.	SVT	_____
47.	VPB	_____
48.	VSD	_____
49.	WPW	_____

7

Lymphatic and Hematic Systems

Learning Objectives

1. Identify the word roots and combining forms relating to the lymphatic and hematic systems.

   Note. You may wish to use Test 7A to evaluate students' knowledge.

	Word Root	Meaning
1.	aden/o	gland
2.	immun/o	resistant
3.	lymph/o	lymph
4.	splen/o	spleen
5.	thym/o	thymus
6.	agglutin/o	clumping
7.	blast/o	primitive cell
8.	coagul/o	clotting
9.	cyt/o	cell
10.	erythr/o	red
11.	granul/o	granules
12.	hem/o	blood
13.	hemat/o	blood
14.	hemoglobin/o	hemoglobin
15.	leuk/o	white
16.	leukocyt/o	white cell
17.	mon/o	one
18.	morph/o	shape
19.	neutr/o	neutral dye
20.	phag/o	eat/swallow
21.	reticul/o	immature
22.	sangui/o	blood
23.	thromb/o	clot
24.	thrombocyt/o	platelet

2. Describe the organs of the lymphatic and hematic systems, and their function.

   Note. You may wish to use Test 7B to assess students' knowledge.

3. Build terms related to this system.

   Note. You may wish to use Test 7C to evaluate students' knowledge.

4. Identify and discuss pathology related to the lymphatic and hematic systems.

   The following pathologic conditions and major disorders are discussed under the lymphatic and hematic systems.

   Note. You may wish to use Test 7D to assess students' knowledge of these conditions.

Major Pathology and Disorders of Lymphatic and Hematic Systems

1. acquired immunodeficiency syndrome (AIDS)
2. AIDS-related complex
3. anaphylactic shock
4. edema
5. elephantiasis
6. Epstein-Barr virus
7. hepatitis-B
8. Hodgkin's disease
9. Kaposi's sarcoma
10. lymphoma
11. lymphangioma
12. lymphosarcoma
13. mononucleosis
14. multiple sclerosis
15. non-Hodgkin's lymphoma
16. pneumocystis carinii
17. sarcoidosis
18. splenomegaly
19. systemic lupus erythematosus
20. thyoma
21. anemia
22. erythroblastosis fetalis
23. hematoma
24. hemolytic disease of the newborn
25. hemophilia
26. polycythemia vera
27. purpura
28. adenoiditis
29. lymphadenitis
30. peritonsillar abscess
31. tonsillitis

5. Name and describe 10 major disorders that relate to the lymphatic and hematic systems.

   Note. You may wish to use Test 7D to evaluate students' knowledge about major disorders.

6. Identify six procedures that pertain to this system.

   Note. You may wish to use Test 7E to assess students' knowledge about major procedures.

   1. lymphadenectomy
   2. lymphoidectomy

3. splenopexy
4. tonsillectomy
5. bone marrow aspiration
6. enzyme-linked immunosorbent assay (ELISA)
7. lymphangiogram
8. Western blot
9. autohemotherapy
10. autologous transfusion
11. homologous transfusion
12. transfusion
13. bleeding time
14. complete blood count
15. differential
16. erythrocyte sedimentation rate
17. hematocrit
18. hemoglobin
19. Monospot
20. prothrombin time
21. red blood count
22. white blood count

7. Interpret abbreviations used in the study of this system.

   Note. You may wish to use Test 7F to evaluate the students' knowledge of abbreviations.

	Abbreviation	Meaning
1.	T8	T-cell lymphocyte
2.	ARC	AIDS-related complex
3.	T4	T-cell lymphocyte
4.	AIDS	acquired immunodeficiency syndrome
5.	NHL	non-Hodgkin's lymphoma
6.	ALL	acute lymphocytic leukemia
7.	mono	mononucleosis, monocyte
8.	AML	acute myelogenous leukemia
9.	lymph	lymphocyte
10.	CD4	protein on T-cell-helper lymphocyte
11.	KS	Kaposi's sarcoma
12.	CGL	chronic granulocytic leukemia
13.	Ig	immunoglobin
14.	CLL	chronic lymphocytic leukemia
15.	HSV	herpes simplex virus
16.	HIV	human immunodeficiency virus
17.	ELISA	enzyme-linked immunosorbent assay
18.	EBV	Epstein-Barr virus
19.	WBC	white blood cell
20.	baso	basophil
21.	RBC	red blood cell
22.	CBC	complete blood count
23.	PT	prothrombin time
24.	eosin	eosinophil
25.	poly	polymorphonuclear neutrophil
26.	ESR	erythrocyte sedimentation rate
27.	PCV	packed cell volume
28.	HgB	hemoglobin

Pronunciation Guide: Lymphatic System

Vocabulary Relating to the Lymphatic System

allergy (AL er je)
allergan (AL er jen)
anaphylaxis (an a fi LAK sis)
antibody (AN ti bod ee)
antigen (AN ti jen)
atypical (a TIP ih kal)
cytotoxic cells (si to TOX ik/cells)
human immunodeficiency virus (human/im u no de FISH en se/virus)
humoral immunity (HYOO mor al/immunity)
immunoglobins (im u no GLOB inz)
lymph (LIMF)
retrovirus (ret ro VI rus)

Common Disorders of the Lymphatic System

adenoiditis (ad e NOYD i tis)
lymphadenitis (lim fad eh NIGH tiz)
peritonsillar abscess (per ih TON si lar/AB ses)
tonsillitis (ton sil I tis)

Pathology Relating to the Lymphatic System

acquired immune deficiency syndrome (AIDS)
anaphylactic shock (an a fi LAK tik/shock)
edema (e DE ma)
elephantiasis (el e fan TI ah sis)
Epstein-Barr virus (Epstein-Barr virus)
hepatitis B (hep a TI tis/B)
Hodgkin's disease (HOJ kins /disease)
Kaposi's sarcoma (KAP oh sez/sar CO ma)
lymphoma (lim FO ma)
lymphangioma (lim fan je OH ma)
lymphosarcoma (lim fo sar KO ma)
mononucleosis (mon o nu kle OH sis)
multiple sclerosis (multiple/skle RO sis)
non-Hodgkin's lymphoma (non-Hodgkin's lymphoma)
pneumocystis carinii (nu mo SIS tis/kar E ne eye)

sarcoidosis (sar koyd O sis)
splenomegaly (sple no MEG ah le)
thyoma (thi O ma)

Procedures Relating to the Lymphatic System

lymphadenectomy (lim fad eh NEK to me)
lymphoidectomy (lim foi DEK to me)
splenopexy (SPLE no pek se)
tonsillectomy (ton sil ECK to me)

Diagnostic and Laboratory Tests of the Lymphatic System

bone marrow aspiration (bone marrow aspiration)
lymphangiogram (lim FAN je oh gram)

PRONUNCIATION GUIDE: HEMATIC SYSTEM

Vocabulary Relating to the Hematic System

agglutination (a gloo ti NA shun)
agranulocytes (a GRAN u lo sitz)
anticoagulant (an ti ko AG u lant)
antihemorrhagic (an ti hem o RAJ ik)
erythrocytes (e RITH ro sitz)
fibrin (FI brin)
fibrinogen (fi BRIN oh jen)
gamma globulin (GAM ah/GLOB u lin)
granulocytes (GRAN u lo sitz)
hemaglobin (he ma GLO bin)
hematocrit (he MAT o krit)
hematology (hem ah TOL oh je)
leukocytes (LOO ko sitz)
phagocyte (FAG oh site)
plasma (PLAZ ma)
platelets (PLAT letz)
prothrombin (pro THROM bin)
Rh factor (Rh factor)
reticulocyte (re TIK u lo site)
serum (SE rum)
serum albumin (SE rum/ al BU min)
serum globulin (SE rum/GLOB u lin)

Pathology Relating to the Hematic System

anemia (a NE me ah)
erythroblastosis fetalis (e rith ro blas TO sis/fe TAL is)
hematoma (he ma TO ma)
hemolytic (he mo LIT ik)
hemophilia (he mo FIL e ah)
polycythemia vera (pol e si THEE me ah/VE rah)
purpura (PUR pu rah)

Procedures Relating to the Hematic System

autohemotherapy (aw to he mo THER ah pe)
autologous transfusion (aw TOL oh gus/trans FU shun)
homologous transfusion (ho MOL oh gus/trans FU shun)

Diagnostic and Laboratory Tests of the Hematic System

differential (dif er EN shal)
erythrocyte (e RITH ro site)
hematocrit (he MAT oh krit)
hemoglobin (hem oh GLO bin)
prothrombin (pro THROM bin)

Name _____ Date _____ Errors _____

Test 7A Identifying Word Roots/Combining Form

Write the definition for the word root/combining form in the space provided.

	Word Root	Definition
1.	aden/o	
2.	immun/o	
3.	lymph/o	
4.	splen/o	
5.	thym/o	
6.	agglutin/o	
7.	blast/o	
8.	coagul/o	
9.	cyt/o	
10.	erythr/o	
11.	granul/o	
12.	hem/o	
13.	hemat/o	
14.	hemoglobin/o	
15.	leuk/o	
16.	leukocyt/o	
17.	mon/o	
18.	morph/o	
19.	neutr/o	
20.	phag/o	
21.	reticul/o	
22.	sangui/o	
23.	thromb/o	
24.	thrombocyt/o	

Name _____ Date _____ Errors _____

Test 7B   Identifying Components of the Lymphatic System

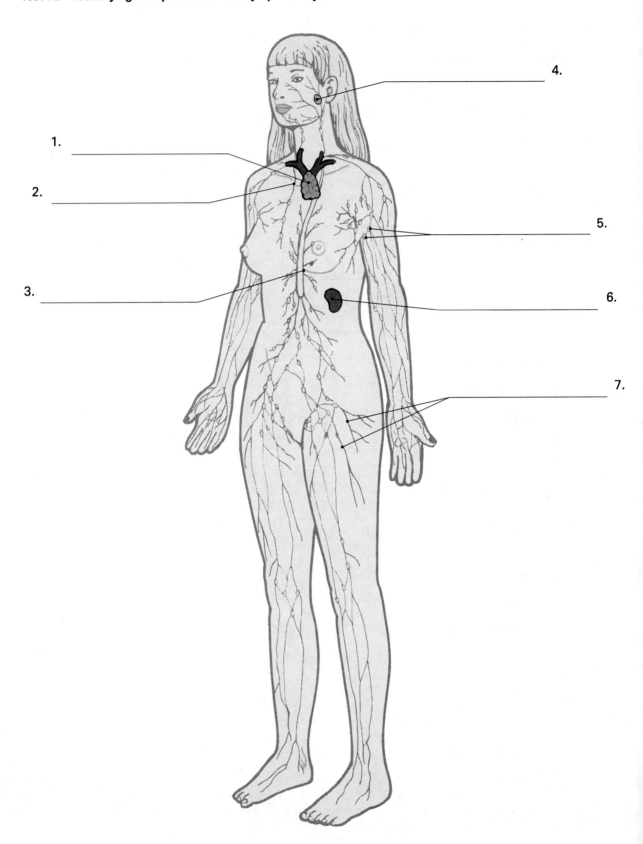

102   INSTRUCTOR'S GUIDE   MEDICAL TERMINOLOGY

Name _____ Date _____ Errors _____

Test 7B Instructor's Answers: Identifying Components of the Lymphatic System

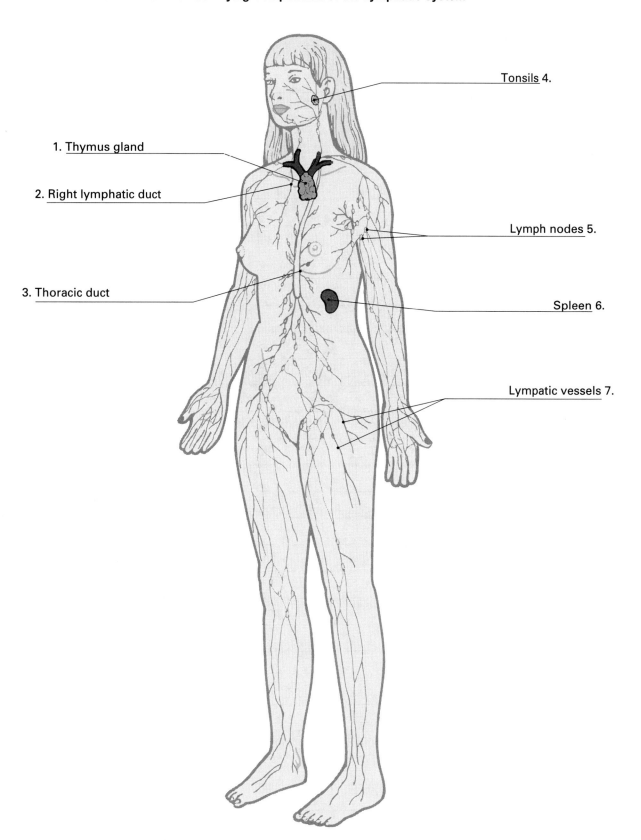

Chapter 7 Lymphatic and Hematic Systems **103**

Name _____ Date _____ Errors _____

Test 7C Building Words for Lymphatic and Hematic Systems

Using prefixes and/or suffixes, create a medical term for the word roots listed below.

	Word Root	New Term Definition
1.	aden/o	
2.	immun/o	
3.	lymph/o	
4.	splen/o	
5.	thym/o	
6.	agglutin/o	
7.	blast/o	
8.	coagul/o	
9.	cyt/o	
10.	erythr/o	
11.	granul/o	
12.	hem/o	
13.	hemat/o	
14.	hemoglobin/o	

	Word Root	New Term Definition
15.	leuk/o	
16.	leukocyt/o	
17.	mon/o	
18.	morph/o	
19.	neutr/o	
20.	phag/o	
21.	reticul/o	
22.	sangui/o	
23.	thromb/o	
24.	thrombocyt/o	

Name _____ Date _____ Errors _____

Test 7D   Define Pathologic Conditions of the Lymphatic and Hematic Systems

Write the definitions for the conditions in the space provided.

1. acquired immune deficiency syndrome (AIDS) _____
   _____

2. AIDS-related complex _____
   _____

3. anaphylactic shock _____
   _____

4. edema _____
   _____

5. elephantiasis _____
   _____

6. Epstein-Barr virus _____
   _____

7. hepatitis B _____
   _____

8. Hodgkin's disease _____
   _____

9. Kaposi's sarcoma _____
   _____

10. lymphoma _____
    _____

11. lymphangioma _____
    _____

12. lymphosarcoma _____
    _____

13. mononucleosis _____
    _____

14. multiple sclerosis _____
    _____

15. non-Hodgkin's lymphoma _____

16. pneumocystis carinii _____

17. sarcoidosis _____

18. splenomegaly _____

19. systemic lupus erythematosus _____

20. thyoma _____

21. anemia _____

22. erythroblastosis fetalis _____

23. hematoma _____

24. hemolytic disease of the newborn _____

25. hemophilia _____

26. polycythemia vera _____

27. purpura _____

28. adenoiditis _____

29. lymphadenitis _____

30. peritonsillar abscess _____

31. tonsillitis _____

Name _____ Date _____ Errors _____

Test 7E Define Major Procedures and Tests of the Lymphatic and Hematic Systems

Procedure/Test Definition

1. lymphadenectomy _____
   _____

2. lymphoidectomy _____
   _____

3. splenopexy _____
   _____

4. tonsillectomy _____
   _____

5. bone marrow aspiration _____
   _____

6. ELISA _____
   _____

7. lymphangiogram _____
   _____

8. Western blot _____
   _____

9. autohemotherapy _____
   _____

10. autologous transfusion _____
    _____

11. homologous transfusion _____
    _____

12. transfusion _____
    _____

13. bleeding time _____
    _____

14. complete blood count _____
    _____

15. differential _____
    _____

16. erythrocyte sedimentation rate _____

17. hematocrit _____

18. hemoglobin _____

19. Monospot _____

20. prothrombin time _____

21. red blood count _____

22. white blood count _____

Name _____ Date _____ Errors _____

Test 7F Definitions of Abbreviations

Write the definition for the abbreviation in the space provided.

	Abbreviation	Definition
1.	T8	_____
2.	ARC	_____
3.	T4	_____
4.	AIDS	_____
5.	NHL	_____
6.	ALL	_____
7.	mono	_____
8.	AML	_____
9.	lymph	_____
10.	CD4	_____
11.	KS	_____
12.	CGL	_____
13.	Ig	_____
14.	CLL	_____
15.	HSV	_____
16.	HIV	_____
17.	ELISA	_____
18.	EBV	_____
19.	WBC	_____
20.	baso	_____
21.	RBC	_____
22.	CBC	_____
23.	PT	_____
24.	eosin	_____
25.	poly	_____
26.	ESR	_____
27.	PCV	_____
28.	HgB	_____

8

Respiratory System

Learning Objectives

1. Identify the word roots and combining forms relating to the respiratory system.

   Note. You may wish to use Test 8A to evaluate students' knowledge.

	Word Root	**Meaning**
1.	thorac/o	lung
2.	bronchi/o	bronchus
3.	trache/o	neck
4.	epiglott/o	epiglottis
5.	rhin/o	nose
6.	laryng/o	larynx
7.	pulmon/o	lung
8.	lob/o	lobe
9.	nas/o	nose
10.	pneumon/o	lung/air
11.	pector/o	chest
12.	pneum/o	lung/air
13.	pharyng/o	pharynx

2. Describe the organs of the respiratory system and their functions.

   Note. You may wish to use Tests 8B and 8C to assess students' knowledge of the organs of the respiratory system.

3. Build terms related to this system.

   Note. You may wish to use Test 8D to assess students' ability to build medical terms related to the respiratory system.

4. Identify and discuss pathology related to the respiratory system.

Note. You may wish to use Test 8E to assess students' knowledge of the pathology and common disorders related to the respiratory system.

Common Disorders and Pathology of Respiratory System

asthma
epistaxis
atelectasis
cystic fibrosis
histoplasmosis
pleural effusion
pneumoniosis
silicosis
tuberculosis
sudden infant death syndrome
respiratory distress syndrome
pneumoncystis carinii
paroxysmal nocturnal dyspnea
hyaline membrane disease
chronic obstructive pulmonary disease
bronchitis

laryngitis
bronchiectasis
emphysema
pleurisy
pneumonia
pneumothorax
tracheostenosis
croup
pertussis
bronchogenic carcinoma
empyema
Legionnaire's disease
pneumonomycosis
pulmonary edema
pulmonary embolism

5. Name and describe 10 major disorders that relate to the respiratory system.

   Note. You may wish to use Test 8E to evaluate students' knowledge.

6. Identify six procedures that pertain to this system.

   Note. You may wish to use Test 8F to assess students' knowledge of the following procedures:

   1. bronchoplasty
   2. bronchoscopy
   3. bronchotomy
   4. cardiopulmonary resuscitation (CPR)
   5. endotracheal intubation
   6. Heimlich maneuver
   7. hyperbaric oxygen therapy
   8. laryngectomy
   9. laryngoplasty
   10. lobectomy
   11. postural drainage
   12. pneumonectomy
   13. rhinoplasty
   14. thoracentesis
   15. thoracostomy
   16. tracheostomy
   17. tracheotomy

7. Interpret abbreviations used in the study of this system.

   Note. You may wish to use Test 8G to evaluate students' knowledge of the following abbreviations:

ABG	A&P	ARD	ARF	BS	CO_2	COLD	COPD	CPR
CTA	CXR	DOE	DPT	ENT	ET	FEF	FEV	FVC
HBOT	HMD	IPPB	IRDS	IRV	LLL	LUL	MBC	MV
MVV	O_2	PCP	PFT	PND	PPD	R	RD	RDS
RLL	RML	RUL	SIDS	SOB	T&A	TB	TLC	TPR
URI	VC	AP view	Broncho	PA view				

Pronunciation Guide: Respiratory System

Vocabulary Relating to the Respiratory System

anoxia (an OK se ah)
anoxemia (an OK se me ah)
asphyxia (as FIK se ah)
hypoxemia (hi POK se me ah)
hypoxia (hi POK se ah)
intubation (in tu BA shun)
spirometer (sp ROM et er)

Diagnostic Terms Relating to the Respiratory System

auscultaton (aws kul TA shun)
Cheyne-Stokes respiration (CHAN/STOKS/respiration)
percussion (per KUSH un)
phlegm (FLEM)
pleural rub (PLOO ral/rub)
purulent (PUR u lent)
rales (RALS)
rhonci (RONG kai)
sputum (SPU tum)
stridor (STRI dor)

Common Disorders Relating to the Respiratory System

asthma (AZ ma)
bronchitis (brong KI tis)
croup (CROOP)
epistaxis (ep ih STAK sis)
laryngitis (lar in JI tis)
pertussis (per TUS is)

Pathology Relating to the Respiratory System

atelectasis (at ee LEK ta sis)
bronchiectasis (brong ke EK ta sis)
bronchogenic carcinoma (brong ko JEN ik/kar si NO ma)
cystic fibrosis (SIS tik/fi BRO sis)
emphysema (em fi SE ma)
histoplasmosis (his to plaz MO sis)
hyaline membrane disease (HI ah lin/membrane disease)
paroxysmal nocturnal dyspnea (par ok SIZ mal/nok TUR nal/disp NE ah)
pertussis (per TUS is)

Chapter 8   Respiratory System   **113**

pleural effusion (PLOO ral/e FU zhun)
pleurisy (PLOO ris e)
pneumonia (nu MO ne ah)
pneumonomycosis (nu mon o mi KO sis)
pneumoniosis (nu mo nee OH sis)
pneumothorax (nu mo THO raks)
pulmonary edema (PUL mo nare re/e DE ma)
pulmonary embolism (PUL mo nare re/EM bo lizm)
silicosis (sil ih KO sis)
tracheostenosis (tra ke o sten O sis)
tuberculosis (tu ber ku LO sis)

Procedures Relating to the Respiratory System

bronchoplasty (BRONG ko plas te)
bronchoscopy (brong KOS ko pe)
bronchotomy (brong KOT o me)
cardiopulmonary resuscitation (kar de o PUL mo ner e/re SUS ih ta shun)
endotracheal intubation (en do TRA ke al/in tu BA shun)
Heimlich maneuver (HEIM lik/maneuver)
hyperbaric oxygen therapy (hi per BEAR ik/oxygen /therapy)
laryngectomy (lar in JECK toh me)
laryngoplasty (lah RING goh plas te)
lobectomy (lo BEK to me)
pneumonectomy (nu mo NEK to me)
rhinoplasty (RI no plas te)
thoracentesis (tho ra sen TE sis)
thoracostomy (tho rah KOS to me)
tracheostomy (tra ke OS to me)
tracheotomy (tra ke OT o me)

Diagnostic and Laboratory Tests of the Respiratory System

bronchography (brong KOG ra fe)
bronchoscopy (brong KOS ko pe)
laryngoscopy (lar IN gos kop e)
pulmonary angiography (PUL mo nare re/an je OG ra fe)
spirometry (spi ROM eh tre)
sputum cytology (SPU tum/si TOL oh je)

Name _____ Date _____ Errors _____

Test 8A Identifying Word Roots/Combining Form

Write the definition of the word root/combining form in the space provided.

	Word Root	Definition
1.	thorac/o	_____
2.	bronchi/o	_____
3.	trache/o	_____
4.	epiglott/o	_____
5.	rhin/o	_____
6.	laryng/o	_____
7.	pulmon/o	_____
8.	lob/o	_____
9.	nas/o	_____
10.	pneumon/o	_____
11.	pector/o	_____
12.	pneum/o	_____
13.	pharyng/o	_____

Test 8B Identifying Components of the Respiratory System

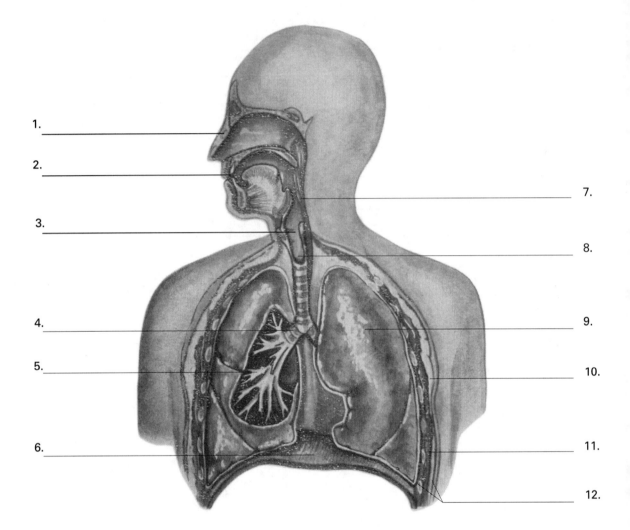

1. _____
2. _____
3. _____
4. _____
5. _____
6. _____
7. _____
8. _____
9. _____
10. _____
11. _____
12. _____

Name _____ Date _____ Errors _____

Test 8B   Instructor's Answers: Components of the Respiratory System

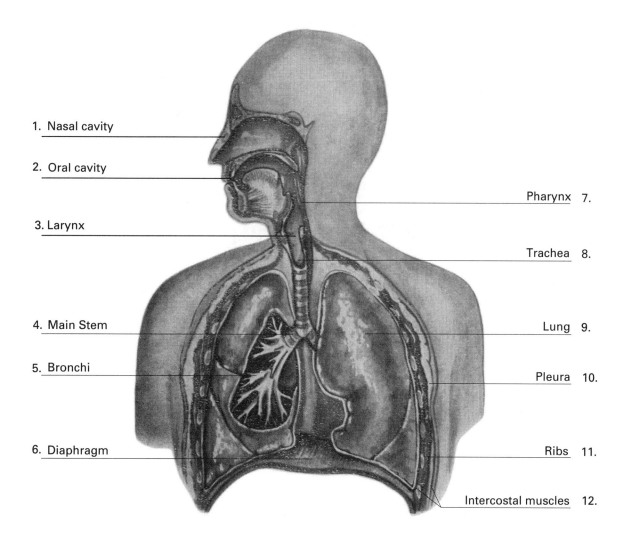

1. Nasal cavity

2. Oral cavity

3. Larynx

4. Main Stem

5. Bronchi

6. Diaphragm

7. Pharynx

8. Trachea

9. Lung

10. Pleura

11. Ribs

12. Intercostal muscles

Chapter 8   Respiratory System   **117**

Name _____ Date _____ Errors _____

Test 8C Identifying Components within the Chest Cavity

CHEST CAVITY

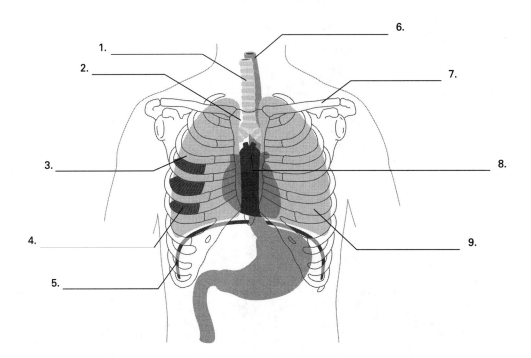

118 INTRUCTOR'S GUIDE MEDICAL TERMINOLOGY

Name _____ Date _____ Errors _____

Test 8C   Instructor's Answers: Components within the Chest Cavity

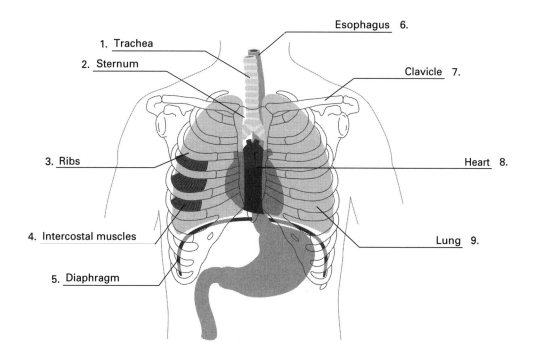

Chapter 8   Respiratory System   **119**

Name _____ Date _____ Errors _____

Test 8D Building Terms Related to the Respiratory System

Using prefixes and/or suffixes, build medical terms in the space provided for each of the word roots/combining forms.

	Word Root	New Term	Definition of Word
1.	thorac/o	_____	_____
2.	bronchi/o	_____	_____
3.	trache/o	_____	_____
4.	epiglott/o	_____	_____
5.	rhin/o	_____	_____
6.	laryng/o	_____	_____
7.	pulmon/o	_____	_____
8.	lob/o	_____	_____
9.	nas/o	_____	_____
10.	pneumon/o	_____	_____
11.	pector/o	_____	_____
12.	pneum/o	_____	_____
13.	pharyng/o	_____	_____

Name _____ Date _____ Errors _____

Test 8E   Common Disorders and Pathology of Respiratory System

Write the definition of the term in the space provided.

1. asthma _____
   _____

2. bronchitis _____
   _____

3. croup _____
   _____

4. epistaxis _____
   _____

5. laryngitis _____
   _____

6. pertussis _____
   _____

7. atelectasis _____
   _____

8. bronchiectasis _____
   _____

9. bronchogenic carcinoma _____
   _____

10. cystic fibrosis _____
    _____

11. emphysema _____
    _____

12. empyema _____
    _____

13. histoplasmosis _____
    _____

14. pleurisy _____
    _____

15. Legionnaire's disease _____
_____

16. pleural effusion _____
_____

17. pneumonia _____
_____

18. pneumonomycosis _____
_____

19. pneumoniosis _____
_____

20. pneumothorax _____
_____

21. pulmonary edema _____
_____

22. silicosis _____
_____

23. tracheostenosis _____
_____

24. pulmonary embolism _____
_____

25. tuberculosis _____
_____

26. sudden infant death syndrome _____
_____

27. respiratory distress syndrome _____
_____

28. Pneumoncystis carinii _____
_____

29. paroxysmal nocturnal dyspnea _____
_____

30. hyaline membrane disease _____
_____

31. chronic obstructive pulmonary disease _____
_____

Name _____ Date _____ Errors _____

Test 8F   Defining Procedures Relating to the Respiratory System

Write the definition of the procedure in the space provided.

1. bronchoplasty _____
   _____

2. bronchoscopy _____
   _____

3. bronchotomy _____
   _____

4. cardiopulmonary resuscitation (CPR) _____
   _____

5. endotracheal intubation _____
   _____

6. Heimlich maneuver _____
   _____

7. hyperbaric oxygen therapy _____
   _____

8. laryngectomy _____
   _____

9. laryngoplasty _____
   _____

10. lobectomy _____
    _____

11. postural drainage _____
    _____

12. pneumonectomy _____
    _____

13. rhinoplasty _____
    _____

14. thoracentesis _____
    _____

15. thoracostomy _____

16. tracheostomy _____

17. tracheotomy _____

Name _____ Date _____ Errors _____

Test 8G Identifying Abbreviations

Write the definition for the abbreviation in the space provided.

1. ABG _____
2. A&P _____
3. ARD _____
4. ARF _____
5. BS _____
6. CO2 _____
7. COLD _____
8. COPD _____
9. CPR _____
10. CTA _____
11. CXR _____
12. DOE _____
13. DPT _____
14. ENT _____
15. ET _____
16. FEF _____
17. FEV _____
18. FVC _____
19. HBOT _____
20. HMD _____
21. IPPB _____
22. IRDS _____
23. IRV _____
24. LLL _____
25. LUL _____
26. MBC _____
27. MV _____
28. MVV _____
29. O2 _____

30. PCP _____
31. PFT _____
32. PND _____
33. PPD _____
34. R _____
35. RD _____
36. RDS _____
37. RLL _____
38. RML _____
39. RUL _____
40. SIDS _____
41. SOB _____
42. T&A _____
43. TB _____
44. TLC _____
45. TPR _____
46. URI _____
47. VC _____
48. AP view _____
49. Broncho _____
50. PA view _____

9

Digestive System

Learning Objectives

1. Identify the word roots and combining forms relating to the digestive system.

    Note. You may wish to use Test 9A to evaluate students' knowledge.

	Word Root	**Meaning**
1.	sigmoid/o	sigmoid colon
2.	aliment/o	nourish
3.	sial/o	saliva
4.	an/o	anus
5.	rect/o	rectum
6.	bil/i	bile
7.	pylor/o	pylorus
8.	bucc/o	cheek
9.	proct/o	rectum
10.	cec/o	cecum
11.	phag/o	eat
12.	cheil/o	lip
13.	pancreat/o	pancreas
14.	chol/e	bile
15.	palat/o	palate
16.	chol/o	bile
17.	or/o	mouth
18.	cholecyst/o	gallbladder
19.	odont/o	tooth
20.	cholangi/o	gallbladder
21.	lingu/o	tongue
22.	choledoch/o	common bile duct
23.	labi/o	lip
24.	col/o	colon
25.	intestin/o	intestine
26.	colon/o	colon
27.	ile/o	ileum

	Word Root	Meaning
28.	cyst/o	cyst/sac
29.	jejun/o	jejunum
30.	dent/o	tooth
31.	hepat/o	liver
32.	duoden/o	duodenum
33.	gloss/o	tongue
34.	enter/o	small intestine
35.	gingiv/o	gums
36.	esophag/o	esophagus
37.	gastr/o	stomach

2. Describe the organs of the digestive system and their function.

    Note. You may wish to use Tests 9B and 9C to assess students' knowledge.

3. Build terms related to this system.

    Note. You may wish to use Test 9D to evaluate students' knowledge.

4. Identify and discuss pathology related to the digestive system.

    Note. You may wish to use Test 9E to assess students' knowledge.

The following terms are discussed in this chapter:

Pathology of the Digestive System

ascites	hepatitis
bulimia	ileitis
cholecystitis	inguinal hernia
cholelithiasis	intussusception
cirrhosis	inflammatory bowel disease
cleft lip	irritable bowel syndrome
cleft palate	jaundice
Crohn's disease	malabsorption syndrome
diverticulitis	peptic ulcer
enteritis	pilonidal cyst
esophageal stricture	polyps
fissure	reflux esophagitis
fistula	ulcerative colitis
gastroenteritis	volvulus

5. Name and describe 10 major disorders that relate to the digestive system.

    Note. You may wish to use Test 9F to evaluate students' knowledge of disorders of the digestive system.

The following terms are discussed in this chapter:

anorexia	gastritis
constipation	halitosis
diarrhea	polyphagia
dyspepsia	regurgitation
emesis	

6. Identify six procedures that pertain to this system.

   Note. You may wish to use Test 9G to assess students' knowledge of the procedures that pertain to this system.

   The following procedures are discussed in this chapter:

anastomosis	appendectomy
cholecystectomy	choledocholithotomy
choledocholithotripsy	colectomy
colostomy	diverticulectomy
esophagogastrostomy	esophagostomy
exploratory laparotomy	fistulectomy
gastrectomy	gastrostomy
glossectomy	hemorrhoidectomy
hepatic lobectomy	ileostomy
jejunoileostomy	jejunostomy
lithotripsy	liver biopsy
proctoplasty	splenectomy
prophylactic measure	vagotomy

7. Interpret abbreviations used in the study of this system.

   Note. You may wish to use Test 9H to evaluate students' knowledge of abbreviations for the digestive system.

	Abbreviation	**Meaning**
1.	h.s.	at bedtime
2.	a.c.	before meals
3.	IBD	inflammatory bowel disease
4.	Ba	barium
5.	IBS	irritable bowel syndrome
6.	BE	barium enema
7.	IV	intravenous
8.	b.i.d.	twice a day
9.	IVC	intravenous cholangiogram
10.	BM	bowel movement
11.	NG	nasogastric (tube)
12.	BS	bowel sounds
13.	NPO	nothing by mouth
14.	CBD	common bile duct
15.	n&v	nausea and vomiting
16.	CHO	carbohydrate
17.	OCG	oral cholecystography
18.	chol	cholesterol
19.	O&P	ova and parasites
20.	CUC	chronic ulcerative colitis
21.	p.c.	after meals
22.	*E. coli*	*Escherichia coli*
23.	PEG	percutaneous endoscopic gastrostomy
24.	EGD	esophagogastroduodenoscopy
25.	P.O.	per os (by mouth)
26.	ERCP	endoscopic retrograde cholangiopancreatography
27.	PP	postprandial
28.	GB	gallbladder

	Abbreviation	Meaning
29.	prn	as required
30.	GI	gastrointestinal
31.	PTC	percutaneous transhepatic cholangiography
32.	HAA	hepatitis-associated antigen
33.	q.d.	daily
34.	HAV	hepatitis A virus
35.	q.i.d.	four times a day
36.	HBIG	hepatitis B immune globulin
37.	RDA	recommended daily allowance
38.	HBV	hepatitis B virus
39.	t.i.d.	three times a day
40.	HCV	hepatitis C virus
41.	TPN	total parenteral nutrition
42.	UGI	upper gastrointestinal (x-ray series)

PRONUNCIATION GUIDE: DIGESTIVE SYSTEM

Common Disorders of the Digestive System

anorexia (an o REK se ah)
constipation kon sti PA shun)
diarrhea (di ah RE ah)
dyspepsia (dis PEP se ah)
emesis (EM e sis)
gastritis (gas TRI tis)
halitosis (hal ih TO sis)
polyphagia (pol e FA je ah)
regurgitation (re gur ji TA shun)

Pathology Relating to the Digestive System

ascites (ah SI tez)
bulimia (bu LIM e ah)
cholecystitis (ko le SIS ti tis)
cholelithiasis (ko le li THI ah sis)
cirrhosis (sir RO sis)
cleft lip (KLEFT/lip)
Crohn's disease (KRONZ/disease)
diverticulitis (di ver tik u LI tis)
enteritis (en ter EYE tis)
esophageal (e sof ah JE al)
fissure (FISH ur)
fistula (FIS tu la)
gastroenteritis (gas troh en ter EYE tis)
ileitis (ill ee EYE tis)

inguinal (ING gwi nal)
intussusception (in tus sus SEP shun)
jaundice (JAWN dis)
peptic ulcer (PEP tik/ulcer)
pilonidal cyst (pi lo NI dal/cyst)
polyps (POL ips)
reflux esophagitis (reflux/e sof ah JI tis)
ulcerative colitis (UL ser a tiv/ko LI tis)
volvulus (VOL vu lus)

Procedures and Surgery Relating to the Digestive System

anastomosis (ah nas to MO sis)
appendectomy (ap en DEK to me)
cholecystectomy (ko le sis TEK to me)
choledocholithotomy (ko led oh ko lith OT to me)
choledocholithotripsy (ko LED oh ko lith oh trip se)
colectomy (ko LEK to me)
colostomy (ko los TO me)
diverticulectomy (di ver tik u LEK to me)
esophagogastrostomy (e sof ah go gas TROS to me)
esophagostomy (e sof ah GOS to me)
exploratory laparotomy (exploratory/lap ar OT to me)
fistulectomy (fis tu LEK to me)
gastrectomy (gas TREK to me)
gastrostomy (gas TROS to me)
glossectomy (glos SEK to me)
hemorrhoidectomy (hem oh roid EK to me)
hepatic lobectomy (he PAT ik/lo BEK to me)
ileostomy (il ee OS to me)
jejunoileostomy (je joo no il ee OS to me)
jejunostomy (je joo NOS to me)
lithotripsy (LITH oh trip se)
liver biopsy (liver/BI op se)
proctoplasty (PROK to plas te)
splenectomy (splee NEK to me)
prophylactic (pro fi LAK tic)
vagotomy (va GOT o me)

Diagnostic and Laboratory Tests of the Digestive System

abdominal ultrasonography (abdominal/ ul trah son OG rah fe)
cholecystogram (ko le SIS to gram)
colonoscopy (ko lon OS ko pe)
endoscopic retrograde cholangiopancreatography (en do SKOP ik/ RET ro grad/ko lan ge oh pan kre ah TOG rah fe)
esophagoscopy (e SOF ah gos ko pe)

gastrointestinal endoscopy (gas tro in TES tin al/en DOS ko pe)
intravenous cholangiogram (in tra VE nus/ko LAN je o gram)
intravenous cholecystography (in tra VE nus/ko le SIS tog ra fe)
occult (uh KULT)
percutaneous transhepatic cholangiography (per ku TA ne us/tranz he PAT ik/ko LAN je og ra fe)
peritoneoscopy (per ih to ne OS ko pe)
laparoscopy (lap ar OS ko pe)
upper gastrointestinal series (upper/gas tro in TES ti nal /series)

Test 9A Identifying Word Roots and Combining Forms for the Digestive System

Write the definition for the word root/combining form in the space provided.

	Word Root	Definition
1.	sigmoid/o	
2.	aliment/o	
3.	sial/o	
4.	an/o	
5.	rect/o	
6.	bil/i	
7.	pylor/o	
8.	bucc/o	
9.	proct/o	
10.	cec/o	
11.	phag/o	
12.	cheil/o	
13.	pancreat/o	
14.	chol/e	
15.	palat/o	
16.	chol/o	
17.	or/o	
18.	cholecyst/o	
19.	odont/o	
20.	cholangi/o	
21.	lingu/o	
22.	choledoch/o	
23.	labi/o	
24.	col/o	
25.	intestin/o	
26.	colon/o	
27.	ile/o	
28.	cyst/o	

	Word Root	Definition
29.	jejun/o	
30.	dent/o	
31.	hepat/o	
32.	duoden/o	
33.	gloss/o	
34.	enter/o	
35.	gingiv/o	
36.	esophag/o	
37.	gastr/o	

Name _____ **Date** _____ **Errors** _____

Test 9B   Identifying Components of the Digestive System

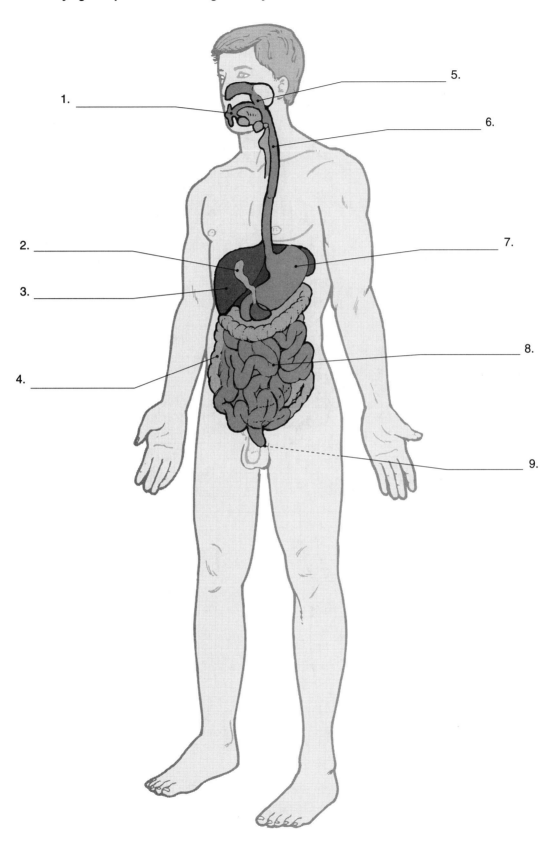

Chapter 9   Digestive System   **135**

Name _____ Date _____ Errors _____

Test 9B Instructor's Answers: Components of the Digestive System

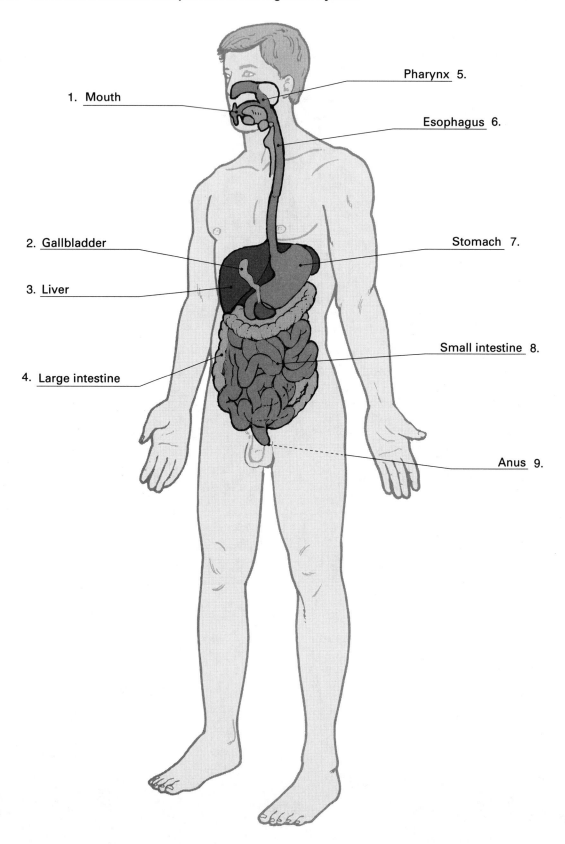

136 INSTRUCTOR'S GUIDE MEDICAL TERMINOLOGY

Name _____ Date _____ Errors _____

Test 9C   Identifying Components of the Tooth

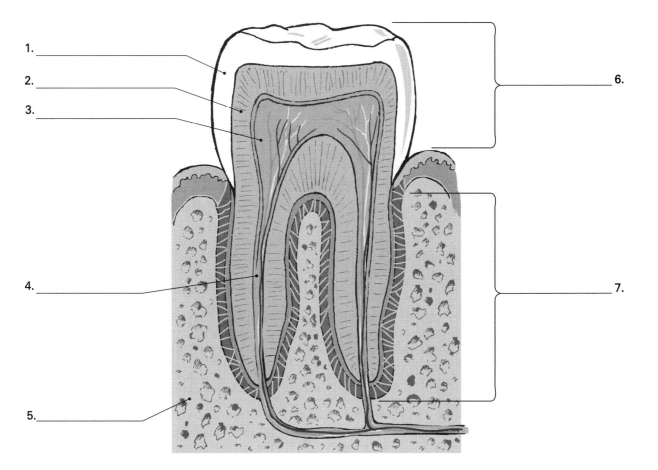

1. _____
2. _____
3. _____
4. _____
5. _____
6. _____
7. _____

Chapter 9   Digestive System   **137**

Name _____ Date _____ Errors _____

Test 9C   Instructor's Answers: Components of the Tooth

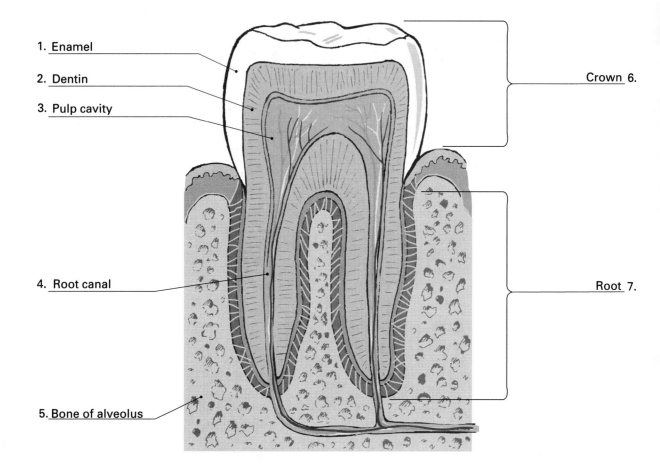

1. Enamel
2. Dentin
3. Pulp cavity
4. Root canal
5. Bone of alveolus
6. Crown
7. Root

Test 9D Building Words for the Digestive System

Using prefixes and/or suffixes, create a medical term for the word roots listed below.

	Word Root	New Term	Definition
1.	sigmoid/o		
2.	aliment/o		
3.	sial/o		
4.	an/o		
5.	rect/o		
6.	bil/i		
7.	pylor/o		
8.	bucc/o		
9.	proct/o		
10.	cec/o		
11.	phag/o		
12.	cheil/o		
13.	pancreat/o		
14.	chol/e		
15.	palat/o		
16.	chol/o		
17.	or/o		
18.	cholecyst/o		
19.	odont/o		
20.	cholangi/o		
21.	lingu/o		
22.	choledoch/o		
23.	labi/o		
24.	col/o		
25.	intestin/o		
26.	colon/o		
27.	ile/o		
28.	cyst/o		

	Word Root	New Term	Definition
29.	jejun/o		
30.	dent/o		
31.	hepat/o		
32.	duoden/o		
33.	gloss/o		
34.	enter/o		
35.	gingiv/o		
36.	esophag/o		
37.	gastr/o		

Name _____ Date _____ Errors _____

Test 9E Define Pathological Conditions of the Digestive System

Write the definition for the condition in the space provided.

1. ascites _____
2. bulimia _____
3. cholecystitis _____
4. cholelithiasis _____
5. cirrhosis _____
6. cleft lip _____
7. cleft palate _____
8. Crohn's disease _____
9. diverticulitis _____
10. enteritis _____
11. esophageal stricture _____
12. fissure _____
13. fistula _____
14. gastroenteritis _____
15. hepatitis _____
16. ileitis _____
17. inguinal hernia _____
18. intussusception _____
19. inflammatory bowel disease _____
20. irritable bowel syndrome _____
21. jaundice _____
22. malabsorption syndrome _____
23. peptic ulcer _____
24. pilonidal cyst _____
25. polyps _____
26. reflux esophagitis _____
27. ulcerative colitis _____
28. volvulus _____

Name _____ Date _____ Errors _____

Test 9F   Defining Major Disorders of the Digestive System

Write the definition for the medical condition in the space provided.

1. regurgitation _____
_____

2. polyphagia _____
_____

3. halitosis _____
_____

4. gastritis _____
_____

5. emesis _____
_____

6. dyspepsia _____
_____

7. diarrhea _____
_____

8. constipation _____
_____

9. anorexia _____
_____

Name _____ Date _____ Errors _____

Test 9G Defining Major Procedures of the Digestive System

Write the definition for the medical procedure in the space provided.

1. vagotomy _____
2. prophylactic measure _____
3. splenectomy _____
4. proctoplasty _____
5. liver biopsy _____
6. lithotripsy _____
7. jejunostomy _____
8. jejunoileostomy _____
9. ileostomy _____
10. hepatic lobectomy _____
11. glossectomy _____
12. gastrostomy _____
13. gastrectomy _____
14. fistulectomy _____
15. explortory laparotomy _____
16. esophagostomy _____
17. esophagogastrostomy _____
18. diverticulectomy _____
19. colostomy _____
20. colectomy _____
21. choledocholithotripsy _____
22. cholecystectomy _____
23. appendectomy _____
24. anastomosis _____

Chapter 9 Digestive System **143**

Name _____ Date _____ Errors _____

Test 9H Definition of Abbreviations

Write the definition for the abbreviation in the space provided.

	Abbreviation	Definition
1.	h.s.	_____
2.	a.c.	_____
3.	IBD	_____
4.	Ba	_____
5.	IBS	_____
6.	BE	_____
7.	IV	_____
8.	b.i.d.	_____
9.	IVC	_____
10.	BM	_____
11.	NG	_____
12.	BS	_____
13.	NPO	_____
14.	CBD	_____
15.	n&v	_____
16.	CHO	_____
17.	OCG	_____
18.	chol	_____
19.	O&P	_____
20.	CUC	_____
21.	p.c.	_____
22.	*E. coli*	_____
23.	PEG	_____
24.	EGD	_____
25.	P.O.	_____
26.	ERCP	_____
27.	PP	_____
28.	GB	_____

Abbreviation	Definition
29. prn	
30. GI	
31. PTC	
32. HAA	
33. q.d.	
34. HAV	
35. q.i.d.	
36. HBIG	
37. RDA	
38. HBV	
39. t.i.d.	
40. HCV	
41. TPN	
42. UGI	

10

Urinary System

Learning Objectives

1. Identify the word roots and combining forms relating to the urinary system.

    Note. You may wish to use Test 10A to evaluate students' knowledge.

	Word Root	Meaning
1.	ur/o	urine
2.	cyst/o	bladder
3.	urin/o	urine
4.	glomerul/o	glomerulus
5.	urethr/o	urethra
6.	lith/o	stone
7.	ureter/o	ureter
8.	nephr/o	kidney
9.	ren/o	kidney
10.	pyel/o	renal pelvis

2. Describe the organs of the urinary system and their function.

    Note. You may wish to use Tests 10B and 10C to assess students' knowledge.

3. State the normal values for urinalysis testing.

    Note. You may wish to use Test 10D to evaluate students' knowledge of normal urinalysis values.

Element	Normal Finding
color	straw colored
odor	aromatic
appearance	clear
specific gravity	1.001–1.030
pH	5.0–8.0
protein	negative to trace

Elements	Normal Findings
glucose	none
ketones	none
occult blood	negative

4. Build terms related to this system.

   Note. You may wish to use Test 10E to assess students' ability to build terms.

5. Identify and discuss pathology related to the urinary system.

   Note. You may wish to use Test 10F to evaluate students' knowledge of pathology related to the urinary system.

   The following terms are discussed in this chapter:

anuria	bladder neck obstruction
diuresis	dysuria
enuresis	glomerulonephritis
hematuria	hydronephrosis
hypospadius	interstitial cystitis
lithotomy	meatotomy
nocturia	phimosis
pyelitis	pyelonephritis
pyuria	renal colic

6. Identify six procedures that pertain to this system.

   Note. You may wish to use Test 10G to assess students' knowledge of the procedures and diagnostic tests relating to the urinary system.

   The following terms are discussed in this chapter:

catheterization	dialysis
hemodialysis	lithotripsy
peritoneal dialysis	renal transplant
clean-catch specimen	cystography
cystoscopy	excretory urography
intravenous pyelogram	urinalysis
urography	

7. Interpret abbreviations used in the study of this system.

   Note. You may wish to use Test 10H to evaluate students' understanding of abbreviations relating to the urinary system.

   The following abbreviations are presented in this chapter:

	Abbreviation	Meaning
1.	UTI	urinary tract infection
2.	ADH	antidiuretic hormone
3.	UC	urine culture
4.	ARF	acute renal failure
5.	U/A	urinalysis
6.	BUN	blood urea nitrogen

	Abbreviation	Meaning
7.	TUR	transurethral resection
8.	CAPD	continuous ambulatory peritoneal dialysis
9.	SG	specific gravity
10.	CC	clean-catch urine specimen
11.	RP	retrograde pyelogram
12.	CL	chloride
13.	pH	acidity or alkalinity of urine
14.	CRF	chronic renal failure
15.	Na	sodium
16.	C&S	culture and sensitivity test
17.	mL	milliliter
18.	cysto	cystoscopy
19.	KUB	kidney, ureter, bladder
20.	ESWL	extracorporeal shock-wave lithotripsy
21.	K	potassium
22.	GU	genitourinary
23.	IVU	intravenous urogram
24.	IVP	intravenous pyelogram
25.	HD	hemodialysis
26.	IPD	intermittent peritoneal dialysis
27.	H_2O	water
28.	I&O	intake and output

PRONUNCIATION GUIDE: URINARY SYSTEM

Word Roots for Urinary System

cystalgia (sis TAL je ah)
cystitis (sis TI tis)
cystocele (SIS toe seal)
cystorrhagia (sis to RA je ah)
nephrectomy (ne FREK to me)
nephritis (nef RI tis)
nephron (NEF ron)
nephromalacia (nef ro ma LAY se ah)
nephropexy (NEF ro peks e)
nephrorrhaphy (nef OR ah fe)
nephrosclerosis (nef ro skle RO sis)
nephrosis (nef RO sis)
nephrotisis (nef ro TI sis)
nephropyosis (nef ro pie O sis)
pyelitis (pi eh LI tis)
pyelonephritis (pi eh lo ne FRI tis)
ureterectasis (u re ter EK ta sis)
ureterorrhagia (u re ter or HA je ah)
ureterostenosis (u re ter oh sten O sis)
urethralgia (u re THRAL je ah)
urethrectomy (u reth EK to me)

urethritis (u re THRI is)
urethroplasty (u re thro PLAS te)
urethrorrhagia (u re thror A je ah)
urethorrhea (u re thror E ah)
urethrostenosis (u re thro sten O sis)

Surgical Terms for the Urinary System

cystectomy (sis TEK to me)
cystolithotomy (sis to li THOT o me)
cystostomy (sis TOS to me)
cystoplasty (SIS to plas te)
lithotripsy (LITH oh trip se)
nephrostomy (ne FROS to me)
pyelolithotomy (pi lo lith OT oh me)
ureterectomy (u re tur ECK to me)
urethropexy (u RE thro peks e)

Terminology Relating to Kidney Stones

calculus (KAL ku lus)
nephrolith (NEF ro lith)
nephrolithiasis (nef ro lith I ah sis)
renal colic (RE nal/KOL ik)
ureterolith (u RE ter oh lith)

Terminology Relating to Urination

anuria (an U re ah)
anuresis (an yur RE sis)
diuresis (di u RE sis)
dysuria (dis U re ah)
enuresis (en u RE sis)
incontinence (in KON ti nenz)
micturition (mik tu RI shun)
nocturia (NOK tu re ah)
oliguria (o lig U re ah)
polyuria (pol e U re ah)
urgency (UR jen se)

Vocabulary Relating to the Urinary System

electrolyte (ee LEK tro lite)
Escherichia coli (esh er IK ee ah/KO lye)
homeostasis (ho me oh STA sis)

osmosis (oz MO sis)
peritoneum (per ih to NE um)
solute (SOL ut)
solvent (SOL vent)
stricture (STRIK chur)
urine (U rin)

Pathology Relating to the Urinary System

glomerulonephritis (glom er u lo ne FRI tis)
hematuria (he muh TUR e ah)
hydronephrosis (hi dro nef RO sis)
hypospadias (hi po SPA de us)
interstitial cystitis (in ter STISH al/sis TI tis)
lithotomy (lith OT oh me)
meatotomy (me ah TOT oh me)
phimosis (fi MO sis)
pyelitis (pi eh LI tis)
pyelonephritis (pi eh lo ne FRI tis)
pyuria (pi U re ah)

Procedures Relating to the Urinary System

catheterization (kath eh ter ih ZA shun)
dialysis (di AL ih sis)
hemodialysis (hem oh di AL ih sis)
lithotripsy (LITH oh trip se)
peritoneal dialysis (per ih to NE al/di AL ih sis)

Diagnostic and Laboratory Tests for the Urinary System

cystography (sis TOG ra fe)
cystoscopy (sis TOS ko pe)
excretory urography (EKS kre to re/U rog ra fe)
intravenous pyelogram (in tra VE nus/PI eh lo gram)
urinalysis (u ri NAL ih sis)
urography (u ROG ra fe)

Name _____ Date _____ Errors _____

Test 10A Identifying Word Roots and Combining Forms

Write the definition for the word root/combining form in the space provided.

	Word Root	Definition
1.	ur/o	_____
2.	cyst/o	_____
3.	urin/o	_____
4.	glomerul/o	_____
5.	urethr/o	_____
6.	lith/o	_____
7.	ureter/o	_____
8.	nephr/o	_____
9.	ren/o	_____
10.	pyel/o	_____

Name _____ Date _____ Errors _____

Test 10B Identifing Components of the Urinary System

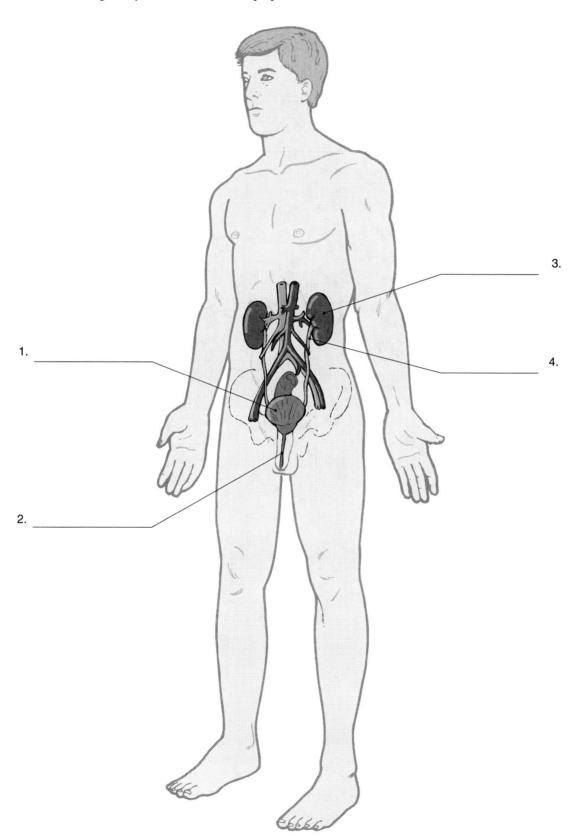

Chapter 10 Urinary System **153**

Test 10B Instructor's Answers: Components of the Urinary System

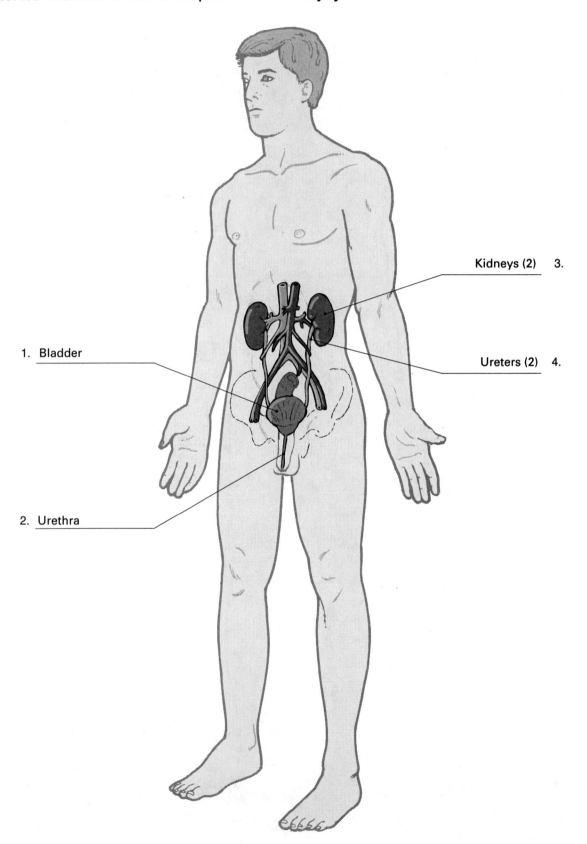

1. Bladder
2. Urethra
3. Kidneys (2)
4. Ureters (2)

Test 10C   Identifying Parts of the Kidney

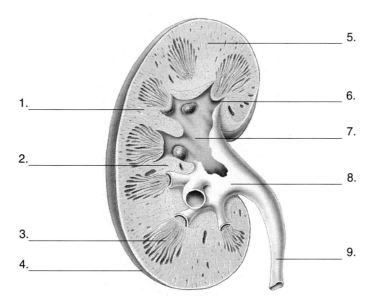

1. _____
2. _____
3. _____
4. _____
5. _____
6. _____
7. _____
8. _____
9. _____

Name _____ Date _____ Errors _____

Test 10C   Instructor's Answers: Parts of the Kidney

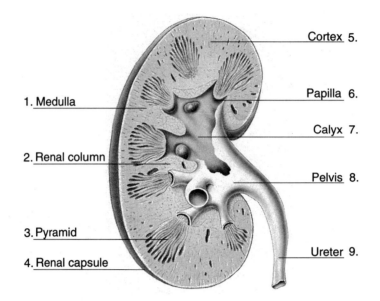

Name _____ Date _____ Errors _____

Test 10D Normal Urinalysis Values

Write the normal values for urinalysis testing in the space provided.

	Element	**Normal Finding**
1.	color	_____
2.	odor	_____
3.	appearance	_____
4.	specific gravity	_____
5.	pH	_____
6.	protein	_____
7.	glucose	_____
8.	ketones	_____
9.	occult blood	_____

Name _____ Date _____ Errors _____

Test 10E Building Words for the Urinary System

Using prefixes and/or suffixes, create a medical term for the word roots listed below.

	Word Root	New Term	Definition
1.	ur/o	_____	_____
2.	cyst/o	_____	_____
3.	urin/o	_____	_____
4.	glomerul/o	_____	_____
5.	urethr/o	_____	_____
6.	lith/o	_____	_____
7.	ureter/o	_____	_____
8.	nephr/o	_____	_____
9.	ren/o	_____	_____
10.	pyel/o	_____	_____

Name _____ Date _____ Errors _____

Test 10F Defining Pathology of the Urinary System

Write the definition of the term in the space provided.

1. anuria _____
2. bladder neck obstruction _____
3. diuresis _____
4. dysuria _____
5. enuresis _____
6. glomerulonephritis _____
7. hematuria _____
8. hydronephrosis _____
9. hypospadius _____
10. interstitial cystitis _____
11. lithotomy _____
12. meatotomy _____
13. nocturia _____
14. phimosis _____
15. pyelitis _____
16. pyelonephritis _____
17. pyuria _____
18. renal colic _____

Name _____ Date _____ Errors _____

Test 10G   Defining Procedures and Diagnostic Tests of the Urinary System

Term   **Definition**

1. catheterization   _____
2. dialysis   _____
3. hemodialysis   _____
4. lithotripsy   _____
5. peritoneal dialysis   _____
6. renal transplant   _____
7. clean-catch specimen   _____
8. cystography   _____
9. cystoscopy   _____
10. excretory urography   _____
11. intravenous pyelogram _____
12. urinalysis   _____
13. urography   _____

Name _____ Date _____ Errors _____

Test 10H Defining Abbreviations of the Urinary System

Write the definition of the abbreviation in the space provided.

	Abbreviation	Definition
1.	UTI	
2.	ADH	
3.	UC	
4.	ARF	
5.	U/A	
6.	BUN	
7.	TUR	
8.	CAPD	
9.	SG	
10.	CC	
11.	RP	
12.	CL	
13.	pH	
14.	CRF	
15.	Na	
16.	C&S	
17.	mL	
18.	cysto	
19.	KUB	
20.	ESWL	
21.	K	
22.	GU	
23.	IVU	
24.	IVP	
25.	HD	
26.	IPD	
27.	H_2O	
28.	I&O	

11

Reproductive System

Learning Objectives

1. Identify the word roots and combining forms relating to the reproductive system.

   Note. You may wish to use Test 11A to evaluate students' knowledge.

	Word Root	**Meaning**
Female Reproductive System		
1.	vulv/o	vulva
2.	cervic/o	neck/cervix
3.	vagin/o	vagina
4.	cervis/o	neck/cervix
5.	uter/o	uterus
6.	colp/o	vagina
7.	umbilic/o	umbilical
8.	epist/o	vulva
9.	salping/o	fallopian tube
10.	galact/o	milk
11.	perine/o	perineum
12.	gravid/o	pregnancy
13.	ov/i	egg
14.	hyster/o	uterus
15.	ovar/i	ovary
16.	lact/o	milk
17.	ov/o	egg
18.	mamm/o	breast
19.	oo/o	egg
20.	mast/o	breast
21.	oophor/o	ovary
22.	men/o	menses/menstruation
23.	nat/a	birth
24.	metr/o	uterus

Word Roots	Meaning

Male Reproductive System

1. andr/o — male
2. vesicul/o — seminal vesicle
3. balan/o — glans penis
4. vas/o — vas deferens
5. epididym/o — epididymis
6. test/o — testes
7. orchid/o — testes
8. spermat/o — sperm
9. orchi/o — testes
10. semin/o — semen
11. prostat/o — prostate
12. orch/o — testes

2. Describe the organs of the reproductive system and their function.

   Note. You may wish to use Tests 11B and 11C to assess students' knowledge.

3. Build terms related to this system.

   Note. You may wish to use Test 11D to evaluate students' knowledge.

4. Identify and discuss pathology related to the reproductive system.

   Note. You may wish to use Test 11E to assess students' knowledge of pathology relating to the reproductive system.

The following pathological conditions are discussed under the reproductive system.

Pathology

abruptio placenta
breech presentation
carcinoma in situ
cervical cancer
cervical polyps
choriocarcinoma
condyloma
cystocele
eclampsia
ectopic pregnancy
endometrial cancer
endometriosis
fibroid tumor
mastitis
ovarian carcinoma
ovarian cyst
pelvic inflammatory disease
placenta previs
pre-eclampsia
premature birth
prolapsed uterus
Rh factor
salpingitis

sexually transmitted disease
spontaneous abortion
stillbirth
toxic shock syndrome
tubal pregnancy

5. Name and describe 10 major disorders that relate to the reproductive system.

   The following pathologic disorders are discussed under the reproductive system. You may wish to use these terms for spelling and pronunciation practice for the students.

   Note. You may wish to use Test 11F to evaluate students' knowledge of common disorders of the male and female reproductive systems.

   amenorrhea
   dysmenorrhea
   menorrhagia
   premenstrual syndrome
   vaginitis
   anorchism
   azoospermia
   benign prostatic hypertrophy (BPH)
   cryptorchidism
   epispadias
   epididymitis
   hydrocele
   hypospadias
   impotent
   perineum
   phimosis
   prostatic hyperplasia
   prostatitis
   varicocele

6. Identify six procedures that pertain to this system.

   Note. You may wish to use Test 11G to assess students' knowledge of procedures of the reproductive system.

   abortion
   cesarean section
   cauterization
   colposcopy
   conization
   contraception
   cryosurgery
   culdoscopy
   dilation and curettage
   episiotomy
   fetal monitor
   hymenectomy
   hysterectomy
   intrauterine device (IUD)
   Kegel exercises
   laparoscopy
   oophorectomy

panhysterectomy
panhysterosalpingo-oophorectomy
pelvic examination
pelvimetry
polypectomy
salpingo-oophorectomy
tubal ligation
castration
circumcision
epididymectomy
orchiectomy
orchidopexy
prostatectomy
sterilization
transurethral resection of the prostate
vasectomy

7. Interpret abbreviations used in the study of this system.

   Note. You may wish to use Test 11H to evaluate students' knowledge.

Abbreviations	Meaning
AH	abdominal hysterectomy
CIS	carcinoma in situ
Cx	cervix
D&C	dilatation and curettage
DUB	dysfunctional uterine bleeding
ECC	endocervical curettage
ERT	estrogen replacement therapy
FSH	follicle-stimulating hormone
gyne	gynecology
HRT	hormone replacement therapy
HSG	hysterosalpingography
HSO	hysterosalpingo-oophorectomy
IUD	intrauterine device
LMP	last menstrual period
MH	marital history
NGU	nongonococcal urethritis
PAP	Pap test
PID	pelvic inflammatory disease
PKU	phenylketonuria
PMP	previous menstrual period
PMS	premenstrual syndrome
TAH	total abdominal hysterectomy
TSS	toxic shock syndrome
AB	abortion
CPD	cephalopelvic disproportion
CS	cesarean section
C-section	cesarean section
CWP	childbirth without pain
DOB	date of birth
EDC	estimated date of confinement
FEKG	fetal electrocardiogram
FHR	fetal heart rate

Abbreviations	Meaning
FHT	fetal heart tones
FTND	full-term normal delivery
grav I	first pregnancy
HCG	human chorionic gonadotropin
HSG	hysterosalpingography
LBW	low birth weight
NB	newborn
OB	obstetrics
para I	first delivery
RML	right mediolateral (episiotomy)
UC	uterine contractions
AIH	artificial insemination homologous
BPH	benign prostatic hypertrophy
GU	genitourinary
PSA	prostate-specific antigen
SPP	suprapubic protatectomy
TUR	transurethral resection
AIDS	acquired immune deficiency syndrome
ARC	AIDS-related complex
HIV	human immunodeficiency virus
HSV	herpes simplex virus
STD	sexually transmitted disease
VD	venereal disease
VDRL	Venereal Disease Research Laboratory

PRONUNCIATION GUIDE: FEMALE REPRODUCTIVE SYSTEM

Vocabulary Relating to the Female Reproductive System

gestation (jes TA shun)
gravida (GRAV ih da)
gynecology (gi ne KOL oh je)
lactation (lack TAY shun)
menopause (MEN oh pawz)
multigravida (mul ti GRAV ih da)
multipara (mul TIP ah ra)
neonate (NE oh nat)
obstetrics (ob STET riks)
postpartum (post PAR tum)
puberty (PU ber te)
puerperium (pu er PE re um)

Common Disorders Relating to the Female Reproductive System

amenorrhea (a men oh RE ah)
dysmenorrhea (dis men oh RE ah)
menorrhagia (men oh RA je ah)

premenstrual syndrome (pre MEN stroo al/syndrome)
vaginitis (vaj in I tis)

Pathology Relating to the Female Reproductive System

abortion (ah BOR shun)
abruptio placenta (a BRUP she oh/pla SEN ta)
carcinoma in situ (kar si NO ma/in/SI tu)
cervical cancer (SER vi kal/Kan ser)
cervical polyps (SER vi kal/POL ipz)
choriocarcinoma (ko re oh kar si NO ma)
cervicitis (ser vi SI tis)
condyloma (kon di LO ma)
eclampsia (e KLAMP se ah)
ectopic pregnancy (ek TOP ik/pregnancy)
endometrial cancer (en do ME tre al/cancer)
endometriosis (en doh me tre OH sis)
fibroid tumor (FI broyd/ tumor)
mastitis (mas TI tis)
multipara (mul TIP a ra)
nullipara (nul IP a ra)
ovarian carcinoma (oh VA re an/kar si NO ma)
ovarian cyst (oh VA re an/sist)
placenta previa (plah SEN tah/PREE ve ah)
preeclampsia (pre e KLAMP se ah)
prolapsed uterus (pro LAPS ed/U ter us)
salpingitis (sal pin JIGH tis)
spontaneous abortion (SPON ta ne us/ah BOR shun)

Procedures Relating to the Female Reproductive System

abortion (ah BOR shun)
cesarean section (see SAY ree an/SECK shun)
cauterization (kaw ter eh ZA shun)
colposcopy (kol POS koh pe)
conization (kon i ZA shun)
contraception (kon tra SEP shun)
cryosurgery (kri o SUR jer ee)
culdoscopy (kul DOS ko pe)
dilation and curettage (dilation/and/ku re TAZH)
episiotomy (eh pee ze OT oh me)
fetal monitor (fetal monitor)
hymenectomy (high men ECK toh me)
hysterectomy (his te REK to me)
Kegel exercises (KE gul/exercises)
laparoscopy (lap ah OS ko pe)

oophorectomy (oh of oh REK to me)
panhysterectomy (pan his ter EK to me)
panhysterosalpingo-oophrectomy (pan his ter oh sal ping go- of oh REK to me)
pelvimetry (pel VIM eh tree)
polypectomy (pol i PEK to me)
salpingo-oophorectomy (sal ping go-of oh REK to me)

Diagnostic and Laboratory Tests of the Female Reproductive System

amniocentesis (am ne oh sen TE sis)
cervical biopsy (SER vi kal/BI op se)
colposcopy (kol POS koh pe)
culdoscopy (kul DOS ko pe)
Doppler ultrasound (DOP lar/UL trah sound)
endometrial biopsy (en do ME tre al/BI op se)
hysterosalpingography (his ter oh sal ping GOG ra fe)
hysteroscopy (his ter OS ko pe)
laparotomy (lap ar OT oh me)
Papanicolaou smear (PAP an ih kel ou/smear)
pelvimetry (pel VIM e tre)
pelvic ultrasonography (PEL vik/ul tra son OG ra fe)

PRONUNCIATION GUIDE: MALE REPRODUCTIVE SYSTEM

Vocabulary of the Male Reproductive System

ejaculation (e jak u LA shun)
intercourse (in TER kors)
spermatogenesis (sper mat oh JEN eh sis)
spermatolytic (sper mat oh LI tik)

Common Disorders of the Male Reproductive System

anorchism (an OR kizm)
azoospermia (a zo oh SPER me ah)
benign prostatic hypertrophy (be NINE/pros TAT ik/hy per TRO fe)
cryptorchidism (kript OR kid izm)
epispadius (ep ih SPA de as)
epididymitis (ep ih did ih MI tis)
hydrocele (HI dro sel)
hypospadius (hi po SPA de as)
impotent (IM po tent)
perineum (per ih NE um)
phimosis (fi MO sis)

prostatic hyperplasia (pros TAT ik/hi per PLA ze ah)
prostatitis (pros ta TI tis)
varicocele (VAR eh ko sel)

Terminology Related to Procedures of the Male Reproductive System

aspermia (a SPER me ah)
balanitis (bal ah NI tis)
carcinoma of the testes (kar si NO ma/of the/ TES tes)
castration (kas TRA shun)
cauterization (kau ter ih ZA shun)
circumcision (ser kum SI shun)
epididymectomy (ep i did ih MEK toe me)
orchiectomy (or ke EK toe me)
orchidopexy (or kid oh PEK se)
prostatectomy (pro sta TEK toe me)
sterilization (ster il i ZA shun)
transurethral resection of the prostate (trans u RE thral/resection/of the prostate)
vasectomy (vah SEK to me)

Sexually Transmitted Diseases in the Male and Female

candidiasis (kan de DI ah sis)
chancroid (SHANG kroyd)
chlamydial infection (kla MID e al/infection)
genital herpes (JEN ih tal/HER pez)
genital warts (JEN ih tal/wortz)
gonorrhea (gon oh RE ah)
hepatitis (hep ah TI tis)
syphillis (SIF eh lis)
trichomoniasis (trik oh mo NI ah sis)
venereal (ve NE re al)

Terminology Related to Genetics

alopecia (al oh PE she ah)
Cooley's anemia (Kooley's/ a NE me ah)
cystic fibrosis (SIS tik/ fi BRO sis)
Down syndrome (Down/ syndrome)
Duchenne muscular dystrophy (du SHEN/mus KU lar/DIS tra fe)
hemophilia (hem oh FIL e ah)
Huntington's chorea (Huntington's/ko RE ah)
retinitis pigmentosa (ret eh NI tis/pig ment TOE sah)
sickle cell anemia (SIK el/cell/a NE me ah)
spina bifida (SPI nah/BIF ah da)
Tay-Sachs disease (TAY/saks/disease)

Test 11 Identifying Word Roots/Combining Form

Write the definition for the word root/combining form in the space provided.

	Word Root	Definition
1.	vulv/o	
2.	cervic/o	
3.	vagin/o	
4.	cervis/o	
5.	uter/o	
6.	colp/o	
7.	umbilic/o	
8.	epist/o	
9.	salping/o	
10.	galact/o	
11.	perine/o	
12.	gravid/o	
13.	ov/i	
14.	hyster/o	
15.	ovar/i	
16.	lact/o	
17.	ov/o	
18.	mamm/o	
19.	oo/o	
20.	mast/o	
21.	oophor/o	
22.	men/o	
23.	nat/a	
24.	metr/o	
25.	andr/o	
26.	vesicul/o	
27.	balan/o	
28.	vas/o	

	Word Root	Definition
29.	epididym/o	
30.	test/o	
31.	orchid/o	
32.	spermat/o	
33.	orchi/o	
34.	semin/o	
35.	prostat/o	
36.	orch/o	

Name _____ Date _____ Errors _____

Test 11B Identifying Organs of the Male and Female Reproductive Systems

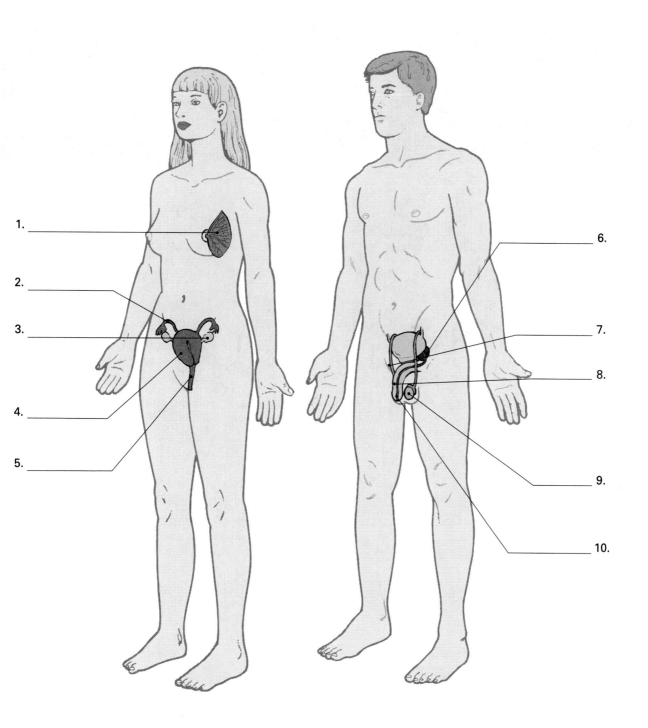

1.
2.
3.
4.
5.
6.
7.
8.
9.
10.

Chapter 11 Reproductive System **173**

Name _____ Date _____ Errors _____

Test 11B   Instructor's Answers: Organs of the Male and Female Reproductive Systems

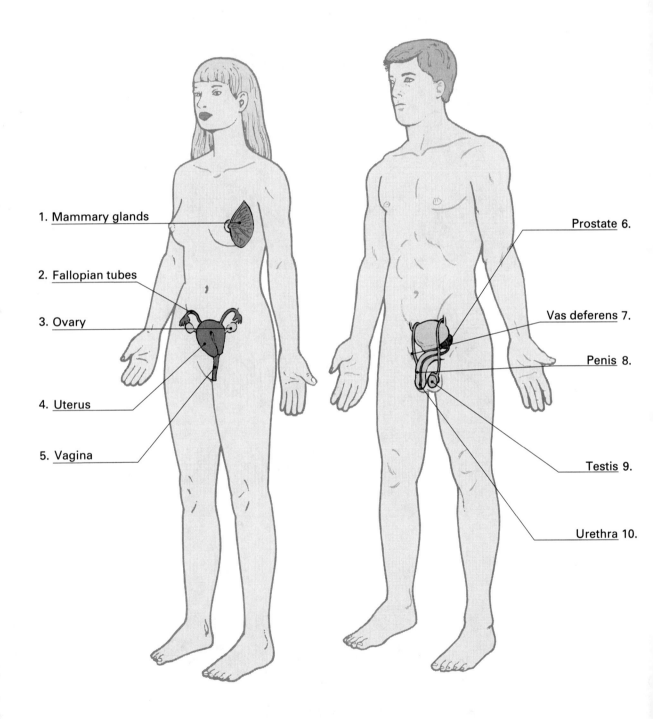

1. Mammary glands
2. Fallopian tubes
3. Ovary
4. Uterus
5. Vagina

6. Prostate
7. Vas deferens
8. Penis
9. Testis
10. Urethra

Name _____ Date _____ Errors _____

Test 11C Identifying Components of the Male Reproductive System

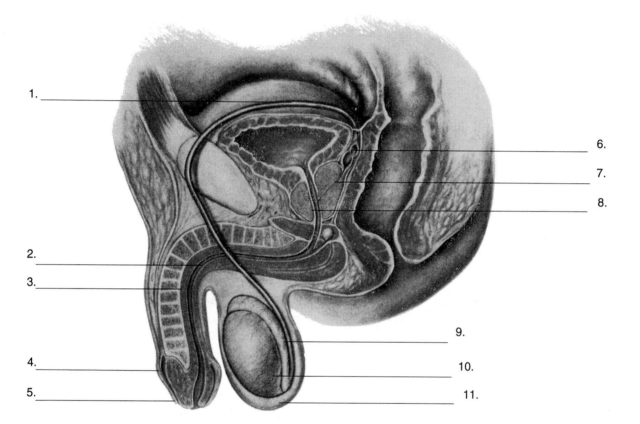

1. _____
2. _____
3. _____
4. _____
5. _____
6. _____
7. _____
8. _____
9. _____
10. _____
11. _____

Chapter 11   Reproductive System   **175**

Name _____ Date _____ Errors _____

Test 11C Instructor's Answers: Components of the Male Reproductive System

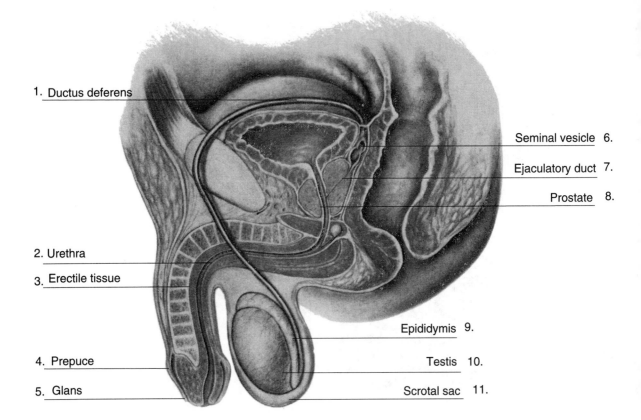

1. Ductus deferens
2. Urethra
3. Erectile tissue
4. Prepuce
5. Glans
6. Seminal vesicle
7. Ejaculatory duct
8. Prostate
9. Epididymis
10. Testis
11. Scrotal sac

Name _____ Date _____ Errors _____

Test 11D Building Words for the Reproductive System

Using prefixes and/or suffixes, create a medical term for the word roots listed below.

	Word Root	New Term	Definition
1.	vulv/o		
2.	cervic/o		
3.	vagin/o		
4.	cervis/o		
5.	uter/o		
6.	colp/o		
7.	umbilic/o		
8.	epist/o		
9.	salping/o		
10.	galact/o		
11.	perine/o		
12.	gravid/o		
13.	ov/i		
14.	hyster/o		
15.	ovar/i		
16.	lact/o		
17.	ov/o		
18.	mamm/o		
19.	oo/o		
20.	mast/o		
21.	oophor/o		
22.	men/o		
23.	nat/a		
24.	metr/o		
25.	andr/o		
26.	vesicul/o		
27.	balan/o		
28.	vas/o		

	Word Root	New Term	Definition
29.	epididym/o		
30.	test/o		
31.	orchid/o		
32.	spermat/o		
33.	orchi/o		
34.	semin/o		
35.	prostat/o		
36.	orch/o		

Name _____ Date _____ Errors _____

Test 11E Defining Pathology Relating to the Reproductive System

1. abruptio placenta _____
2. breech presentation _____
3. carcinoma in situ _____
4. cervical cancer _____
5. cervical polyps _____
6. choriocarcinoma _____
7. condyloma _____
8. cystocele _____
9. eclampsia _____
10. ectopic pregnancy _____
11. endometrial cancer _____
12. endometriosis _____
13. fibroid tumor _____
14. mastitis _____
15. ovarian carcinoma _____
16. ovarian cyst _____
17. pelvic inflammatory disease _____
18. placenta previs _____
19. pre-eclampsia _____
20. premature birth _____
21. prolapsed uterus _____
22. Rh factor _____
23. salpingitis _____
24. sexually transmitted disease _____
25. spontaneous abortion _____
26. stillbirth _____
27. toxic shock syndrome _____
28. tubal pregnancy _____

Name _____ Date _____ Errors _____

Test 11F   Defining Common Disorders of the Female and Male Reproductive Systems

Write the definition of the medical condition in the space provided.

1. amenorrhea _____
2. dysmenorrhea _____
3. menorrhagia _____
4. premenstrual syndrome _____
5. vaginitis _____
6. anorchism _____
7. azoospermia _____
8. benign prostatic hypertrophy (BPH) _____
9. cryptorchidism _____
10. epispadias _____
11. epididymitis _____
12. hydrocele _____
13. hypospadias _____
14. impotent _____
15. perineum _____
16. phimosis _____
17. prostatic hyperplasia _____
18. prostatitis _____
19. varicocele _____

Name _____ Date _____ Errors _____

Test 11G Define Procedures for the Reproductive System.

Write the definition for the procedure in the space provided.

1. cesarean section _____
   _____

2. cauterization _____
   _____

3. colposcopy _____
   _____

4. conization _____
   _____

5. contraception _____
   _____

6. cryosurgery _____
   _____

7. culdoscopy _____
   _____

8. dilation and curettage _____
   _____

9. episiotomy _____
   _____

10. fetal monitor _____
    _____

11. hymenectomy _____
    _____

12. hysterectomy _____
    _____

13. IUD _____
    _____

14. Kegel exercises _____
    _____

15. laparoscopy _____
    _____

16. oophorectomy _____

17. panhysterectomy _____

18. panhysterosalpingo-oophorectomy _____

19. pelvic examination _____

20. pelvimetry _____

21. polypectomy _____

22. salpingo-oophorectomy _____

23. tubal ligation _____

24. castration _____

25. circumcision _____

26. epididymectomy _____

27. orchiectomy _____

28. orchidopexy _____

29. prostatectomy _____

30. sterilization _____

31. transurethral resection of the prostate _____

32. vasectomy _____

Name _____ Date _____ Errors _____

Test 11H Defining Abbreviations

Write the definition for the abbreviation in the space provided.

1. AH _____
2. CIS _____
3. Cx _____
4. D & C _____
5. DUB _____
6. ECC _____
7. ERT _____
8. FSH _____
9. gyne _____
10. HRT _____
11. HSG _____
12. HSO _____
13. IUD _____
14. LMP _____
15. MH _____
16. NGU _____
17. PAP _____
18. PID _____
19. PKU _____
20. PMP _____
21. PMS _____
22. TAH _____
23. TSS _____
24. AB _____
25. CPD _____
26. CS _____
27. C-section _____
28. CWP _____
29. DOB _____

30. EDC _____
31. FEKG _____
32. FHR _____
33. FHT _____
34. FTND _____
35. grav I _____
36. HCG _____
37. HSG _____
38. LBW _____
39. NB _____
40. OB _____
41. para I _____
42. RML _____
43. UC _____
44. AIH _____
45. BPH _____
46. GU _____
47. PSA _____
48. SPP _____
49. TUR _____
50. AIDS _____
51. ARC _____
52. HIV _____
53. HSV _____
54. STD _____
55. VD _____
56. VDRL _____

12

Nervous System

Learning Objectives

1. Identify the word roots and combining forms relating to the nervous system.

   Note. You may wish to use Test 12A to evaluate students' knowledge.

Word Root	Meaning
vag/o	vagus nerve
cephal/o	head
spondyl/o	vertebra
cerebell/o	cerebellum
radicul/o	nerve root
cerebr/o	brain
psych/o	mind
crani/o	head, skull
poli/o	gray
dur/o	hard
phas/o	speech
encephal/o	brain
neur/o	nerve
gangli/o	ganglion
myel/o	spinal cord
ganglion/o	ganglion
meningi/o	meninges
gli/o	glue
mening/o	meninges
medull/o	medulla

2. Describe the organs of the nervous system and their function.

   Note. You may wish to use Test 12B to assess students' knowledge.

3. Build terms related to this system.

    Note. You may wish to use Test 12C to evaluate students' ability to build words.

4. Identify and discuss pathology related to the nervous system.

    The following terms are discussed in this chapter. You may wish to use these terms to test the students' spelling and pronunciation skills.

    Pathology for the Nervous System

    Alzheimer's disease
    amyotropic lateral sclerosis (ALS)
    anorexia nervosa
    asthenia
    ataxia
    Bell's palsy
    cerebrovascular accident (CVA)
    chorea
    concussion
    craniocele
    dementia
    embolism
    encephalocele
    epidural hematoma
    glioma
    hematoma
    herniated nucleus pulposa
    Huntington's chorea
    meningioma
    multiple sclerosis (MS)
    myasthenia gravis
    neuritis
    neurosis
    paralysis
    Parkinson's disease
    pica
    quadriplegia
    seizure
    sleep disorder
    subdural hematoma
    tetraplegia
    transient ischemic attack

    amnesia
    aneurysm
    aphasia
    astrocytoma
    autism
    brain tumor
    cerebral palsy (CP)
    coma
    convulsion
    delirium
    dysphasia
    encephalitis
    encephalosclerosis
    epilepsy
    grand mal
    hemiparesis
    hemiplegia
    hydrocephalus
    meningitis
    meningocele
    narcolepsy
    neuroblastoma
    palsy
    paraplegia
    petit mal
    psychosis
    Reye's syndrome
    shingles
    spina bifida
    syncope
    tic douloureaux

5. Identify six procedures that pertain to this system.

    Note. You may wish to use Test 12D to assess students' understanding of procedures and diagnostic tests.

    Procedures and Diagnostic Tests

    transcutaneous electrical nerve stimulation (TENS)
    spinal puncture
    Romberg's sign

positron emission tomography (PET)
pneumoencephalography
myelography
magnetic resonance imaging (MRI)
lumbar puncture (LP)
electromyogram (EMG)
electroencephalography (EEG)
echoencephalography
cerebrospinal fluid analysis (CSF)
computerized axial tomography (CAT, CT)
cerebral angiography
Babinski's sign
vagotomy
trephination
sympathectomy
nerve block
laminectomy
cryosurgery
craniotomy
cordectomy
cerebrospinal fluid shunts
carotid endarterectomy
brain scan

6. Interpret abbreviations used in the study of this system.

   Note. You may wish to use Test 12E to evaluate the students' understanding of abbreviations.

Abbreviation	Meaning
ALS	amyotropic lateral sclerosis
ANS	autonomic nervous system
CAT, CT	computerized axial tomography
CNS	central nervous system
CP	cerebral palsy
CSF	cerebrospinal fluid
CVA	cerebrovascular accident
EEG	electroencephalogram
EMG	electromyogram
EST	electric shock therapy
HNP	herniated nucleus pulposa (herniated disk)
LP	lumbar puncture
MRI	magnetic resonance imaging
MS	multiple sclerosis
PEG	pneumoencephalogram
PET	positron emission tomography
PNS	peripheral nervous system
TENS	transcutaneous electrical nerve stimulation
TIA	transient ischemic attack

PRONUNCIATION GUIDE: THE NERVOUS SYSTEM

THE CRANIAL NERVES

olfactory (ol FAK to re)
optic (OP tik)
oculomotor (ok u lo MO tur)
trochlear (TROK le ar)
trigeminal (tri JEM in al)
abducens (ab DU sens)
facial (FA shal)
acoustic (ah KOOS tik)
glossopharyngeal (glos oh fa RIN je al)
vagus (VA gus)
spinal accessory (spinal accessory)
hypoglossal (hi po GLOS al)

Vocabulary Relating to the Nervous System

anesthesia (an es THE ze ah)
astrocyte (as TRO site)
conscious (KON shus)
grand mal (GRAN mul)
idiopathic (id e o PATH ik)
lethargy (LETH ar je)
neurology (nu ROL oh je)
neurologist (nu ROL oh jist)
petit mal (pet E/mal)
psychiatrist (si KI ah trist)
psychiatry (si KI ah tre)
psychology (si KOL oh je)
psychologist (si KOL oh jist)
psychosomatic (si ko so MAT ik)
unconscious (un KON shus)

Pathology Relating to the Nervous System

Alzheimer's disease (ALTS hi merz/ disease)
amnesia (am NE ze ah)
amyotrophic lateral sclerosis (a mi o TROF ik/lat ER al/skle RO sis)
aneurysm (AN u rizm)
anorexia nervosa (an oh REK se ah/ner VO sa)
aphasia (a FA ze a)
asthenia (as THE ne ah)
astrocytoma (as tro si TO ma)

ataxia (a TAK se ah)
autism (aw TIZM)
Bell's palsy (Bell's/ PAWL ze)
cerebral palsy (SER eh bral/PAWL ze)
cerebrovascular accident (ser e bro VAS ku lar/accident)
chorea (ko RE ah)
concussion (kon KUSH un)
convulsion (kon VUL shun)
craniocele (KRA ne oh seal)
delerium (de LIR e um)
dementia (de MEN she ah)
dysphasia (dis FA ze ah)
embolism (EM bo lizm)
encephalitis (en sef ah LI tis)
encephalocele (en SEF ah lo seal)
encephalosclerosis (en sef a lo skle RO sis)
epidural hematoma (ep eh DU ral/hem ah TO ma)
epilepsy (EP eh lep se)
glioma (gli O ma)
grand mal (GRAN/MAL)
hematoma (hem ah TO ma)
hemiparesis (hem e PAR e sis)
hemiplegia (hem e PLE je ah)
herniated nucleus pulposa (her ne ATE ed/NU kle us/pul PO sa)
Huntington's chorea (Huntington's/ko RE ah)
hydrocephalus (hi dro SEF ah lus)
meningioma (men in ji O ma)
meningitis (men in JI tis)
meningocele (men IN go seal)
narcolepsy (nar ko LEP se)
neuritis (nu RI tis)
neuroblastoma (nu ro blas TO ma)
neurosis (nu RO sis)
palsy (PAWL ze)
paralysis (pa RAL eh sis)
paraplegia (par ah PLE je ah)
Parkinson's disease (Parkinson's /disease)
pica (PYE ka)
psychosis (si KO sis)
quadriplegia (kwod re PLE je ah)
Reye's syndrome (RIZ/syndrome)
seizure (SE zhur)
spina bifida (SPI nah / BIF eh dah)
subdural hematoma (sub DU ral/ hem ah TO ma)
syncope (SIN co pe)
tetraplegia (te tra PLE je ah)
tic douloureux (TICK/do loo ROO)
transient ischemic attack (TRANS shent/is KE mik/attack)

Procedures Relating to the Nervous System

carotid endarterectomy (ka ROT id/end ar ter EK to me)
cerebrospinal (ser e bro SPI nal)
cordectomy (kor DEK to me)
craniotomy (kra ne OT oh me)
cryosurgery (kri oh SER jer ee)
laminectomy (lam eh NEK to me)
sympathectomy (sim pah THEK to me)
trephination (tref eh NA shun)
vagotomy (va GOT oh me)

Diagnostic and Laboratory Tests of the Nervous System

Babinski's sign (ba BIN skez/sign)
cerebral angiogrphy (ser E bral/an je OG ra fe)
cerebrospinal fluid analysis (ser e bro SPI nal/ fluid/analysis)
echoencephalography (ek oh in SEF ah log ra fe)
electroencephalography (e lek tro en SEF ah log ra fe)
electromyogram (e lek tro MI oh gram)
lumbar puncture (lumbar puncture)
myelography (mi e LOG ra fe)
pneumoencephalography (nu mo en sef ah LOG ra fe)
positron emission tomography (POZ ih tron/E mish on/tom OG ra fe)
Romberg's sign (ROM bergs/sign)
transcutaneous electrical nerve stimulation (trans que TA ne us/electrical/nerve/ stimulation)

Name _____ Date _____ Errors _____

Test 12A Identifying Word Roots/Combining Form

Write the definition for the term in the space provided.

	Word Root	Definition
1.	vag/o	
2.	cephal/o	
3.	spondyl/o	
4.	cerebell/o	
5.	radicul/o	
6.	cerebr/o	
7.	psych/o	
8.	crani/o	
9.	poli/o	
10.	dur/o	
11.	phas/o	
12.	encephal/o	
13.	neur/o	
14.	gangli/o	
15.	myel/o	
16.	ganglion/o	
17.	meningi/o	
18.	gli/o	
19.	mening/o	
20.	medull/o	

Name _____ Date _____ Errors _____

Test 12B   Identifying Components of the Brain

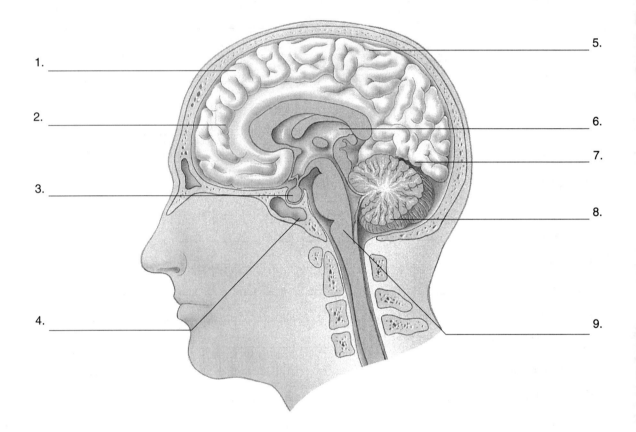

1. _____
2. _____
3. _____
4. _____
5. _____
6. _____
7. _____
8. _____
9. _____

Name _____ Date _____ Errors _____

Test 12B   Instructor's Answers: Components of the Brain

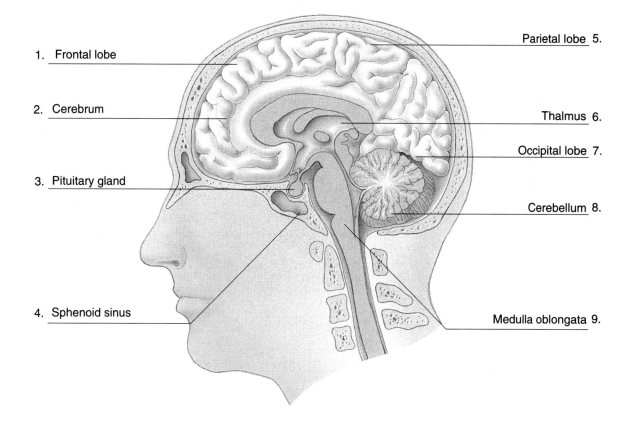

1. Frontal lobe
2. Cerebrum
3. Pituitary gland
4. Sphenoid sinus
5. Parietal lobe
6. Thalmus
7. Occipital lobe
8. Cerebellum
9. Medulla oblongata

Name _____ Date _____ Errors _____

Test 12C Building Words for the Nervous System

Using prefixes or suffixes, create a medical term for the word roots listed below.

	Word Root	New Term	Definition
1.	vag/o	_____	_____
2.	cephal/o	_____	_____
3.	spondyl/o	_____	_____
4.	cerebell/o	_____	_____
5.	radicul/o	_____	_____
6.	cerebr/o	_____	_____
7.	psych/o	_____	_____
8.	crani/o	_____	_____
9.	poli/o	_____	_____
10.	dur/o	_____	_____
11.	phas/o	_____	_____
12.	encephal/o	_____	_____
13.	neur/o	_____	_____
14.	gangli/o	_____	_____
15.	myel/o	_____	_____
16.	ganglion/o	_____	_____
17.	meningi/o	_____	_____
18.	gli/o	_____	_____
19.	mening/o	_____	_____
20.	medull/o	_____	_____

Name _____ Date _____ Errors _____

Test 12D Defining Procedures and Diagnostic Tests of the Nervous System

Write the definition for the term in the space provided.

1. transcutaneous electrical nerve stimulation (TENS) _____

2. spinal puncture _____

3. Romberg's sign _____

4. positron emission tomography (PET) _____

5. pneumoencephalography _____

6. myelography _____

7. magnetic resonance imaging (MRI) _____

8. lumbar puncture (LP) _____

9. electromyogram (EMG) _____

10. electroencephalography (EEG) _____

11. echoencephalography _____

12. cerebrospinal fluid analysis (CSF) _____

13. computerized axial tomography (CAT, CT) _____

14. cerebral angiography _____

15. Babinski's sign _____

16. vagotomy _____

17. trephination _____

18. sympathectomy _____

19. nerve block _____

20. laminectomy _____

21. cryosurgery _____

22. craniotomy _____

23. cordectomy _____

24. cerebrospinal fluid shunts _____

25. carotid endarterectomy _____

26. brain scan _____

Test 12E Defining Abbreviations

Write the definition for the abbreviation in the space provided.

	Abbreviation	Definition
1.	ALS	
2.	ANS	
3.	CAT, CT	
4.	CNS	
5.	CP	
6.	CSF	
7.	CVA	
8.	EEG	
9.	EMG	
10.	EST	
11.	HNP	
12.	LP	
13.	MRI	
14.	MS	
15.	PEG	
16.	PET	
17.	PNS	
18.	TENS	
19.	TIA	

13
Special Senses

Learning Objectives

1. Identify the word roots and combining forms relating to the special senses.

    Note. You may wish to use Test 13A to evaluate students' understanding of the word roots and combining form.

Word Root	Meaning
aque/o	water
blephar/o	eyelid
acous/o	hearing
conjunctiv/o	conjunctiva
cor/o	pupil
audi/o	hearing
corne/o	cornea
cycl/o	ciliary muscle
audit/o	hearing
dacry/o	tear, tear duct
ir/o	iris
auricul/o	ear
irid/o	iris
kerat/o	cornea
lacrim/o	tears
ocul/o	eye
cochle/o	cochlea
ophthalm/o	eye
mastoid/o	mastoid process
opt/o	eye, vision
myring/o	eardrum
optic/o	eye
ot/o	ear
pupil/o	pupil
staped/o	stapes
retin/o	retina

Word Root	Meaning
tympan/o	eardrum, middle ear
scler/o	sclera
uve/o	vascular
vitre/o	glassy

2. Describe the organs of the special senses and their function.

   Note. You may wish to use Tests 13B and 13C to assess students' understanding of anatomy for the special senses.

3. Build terms related to this system.

   Note. You may wish to use TEST 13D to evaluate students' ability to build medical terms.

4. Identify and discuss pathology related to the special senses.

   Note. You may wish to use Test 13E to assess students' understanding of pathology relating to the special senses.

Pathology

cataract	chalazion
diabetic retinopathy	ectropion
entropion	glaucoma
hordeolum	keratitis
macular degeneration	retinal detachment
retinitis pigmentosa	strabismus
trachoma	acoustic neuroma
anacusis	Meniere's disease
otitis media	presbyacusis

5. Name and describe 10 major disorders that relate to the special senses.

   Note. You may wish to use Test 13F to evaluate the students' understanding of disorders pertaining to the special senses.

Disorders

achromatopsia	astigmatism
blepharitis	blepharochalasis
conjunctivitis	esotropia
exophthalmus	exotropia
hemianopia	hyperopia
myopia	nystagmus
presbyopia	

6. Identify six procedures that pertain to this system.

   Note. You may wish to use Test 13G to assess students' understanding of procedures and diagnostic tests.

Procedures and Diagnostic Tests

fluorescein angiography	laser surgery
slit-lamp microscope	vitrectomy
color vision test	gonioscopy
keratometry	ophthalmoscopy
Snellen chart	tonometry
visual acuity test	mastoid antrotomy

myringoplasty	myringotomy
otoplasty	otoscopy
stapedectomy	tympanoplasty
audiogram	audiometric
falling test	mastoid
Rinne and Weber tuning-fork tests	tympanometry

7. Interpret abbreviations used in the study of this system.

   Note. You may wish to use Test 13H to evaluate the students' knowledge of abbreviations relating to the special senses.

Abbreviation	Meaning
Acc.	accommodation
ARMD	age-related macular degeneration
Astigm.	astigmatism
c.gl.	correction with glasses
cyl.	cylindrical lens
D	diopter (lens strength)
DVA	distance visual acuity
ECCE	extracapsular cataract extraction
EM	emmetropia (normal vision)
EOM	extraocular movement
ICCE	intracapsular cataract cryoextraction
IOL	intraocular lens
IOP	intraocular pressure
L & A	light and accommodation
LE	left eye
MY	myopia
NVA	near visual acuity
OD	right eye (oculus dexter)
Ophth.	ophthalmology
OS	left eye (oculus sinister)
OU	each eye
PERLA	pupils equal, react to light and accommodation
RE	right eye
REM	rapid eye movement
s. gl.	without correction or glasses
SMD	senile macular degeneration
VA	visual acuity
VF	visual field
+	plus/convex
-	minus/concave
AC	air conduction
AD	right ear (O)
AS	left ear (X)
AU	both ears
BC	bone conduction
dB	decibel
ENT	ear, nose, and throat
EENT	eyes, ears, nose, and throat
OM	otitis media
Oto	otology
PE tube	polyethylene tube placed in eardrum
UCHD	usual childhood diseases

PRONUNCIATION GUIDE: SPECIAL SENSES—EYES

Vocabulary Relating to the Action of the Eye

accommodation (a kom oh DA shun)
convergence (kon VER jens)
emmetropia (em eh TRO pe ah)
refraction (re FRAK shun)
refractive error (re FRAK tiv/error)

Common Disorders of the Eye

achromatopsia (ah kro mah TOP se ah)
astigmatism (a STIG ma tizm)
blepharitis (blef ar I tis)
blepharochalsis (blef ah ro CHAL sis)
conjunctivitis (kon junk ti VI tis)
esotropia (es o TROH pe ah)
exophthalmus (ek sof THAL mus)
exotropia (ek so TROH pe ah)
hemianopia (hem ee ah NO pe ah)
hyperopia (hi per O pe ah)
myopia (my OH pe ah)
nystagmus (nis TAG mus)
presbyopia (pres be O pe ah)

Pathology Relating to the Eye

cataract (CAT ah ract)
chalazion (ka LA zi on)
diabetic retinopathy (di ah BET ik/ret ih NOP ah thee)
ectropion (ek TRO pe on)
entropion (en TRO pe on)
glaucoma (glaw KO ma)
hordeolum (hor DEE oh lum)
keratitis (ker ah TIE tis)
macular (MAK u lar)
retinal detachment (RET eh nal/ detachment)
retinitis pigmentosa (ret in I tis/pig men TO sa)
strabismus (tra BIZ mus)
trachoma (tra KO ma)

Procedures Relating to the Eye

fluorescein angiography (floo/ oh RES e in/an je OG ra fe)
laser surgery (LA zer/ surgery)
slit-lamp microscope (slit-lamp/microscope)
vitrectomy (vi TREK to me)

Diagnostic and Laboratory Tests Relating to the Eye

gonioscopy (go NE os ko pe)
keratometry (ker ah TOM eh tre)
ophthalmoscopy (of thal MOS ko pe)
Snellen chart (SNEL en/chart)
tonometry (ton OM e try)
visual acuity (VIZH u al/ah KU ih te)

PRONUNCIATION GUIDE: SPECIAL SENSES—EARS

Vocabulary Relating to the Ear

conductive hearing loss (conductive hearing loss)
cerumen (se ROO men)
eustachian (u STA shen)
otorhinolaryngology (o to ri no lar in GOL o je)
sensorineural (sen su re NEW ral)
vestibular (ves TIB u lar)

Pathology Relating to the Ear

acoustic neuroma (a KU stik/ nu RO ma)
anacusis (an ah KU sis)
Meniere's disease (mane ERZ/disease)
otitis media (O TI tis/ media)
otosclerosis (o to skle RO sis)
presbycusis (pres bi KU sis)

Procedures Relating to the Ear

mastoid antrotomy (MAS toid /an TROT oh me)
myringoplasty (mi RING go plas te)

Chapter 13 Special Senses   203

myringotomy (mir in GOT o me)
otoplasty (O to plas te)
otoscopy (O TOS ko pe)
stapedectomy (sta pe DEK to me)
tympanoplasty (tim pah no PLAS te)

Diagnostic and Laboratory Tests Relating to the Ear

audiogram (AW de o gram)
audiometric (aw de o MET rik)
mastoid (mas TOID)
otoscopy (o TOS ko pe)
tympanometry (tim pan NOM eh tre)

Name _____ Date _____ Errors _____

Test 13A Defining Word Roots/Combining Forms

Write the definition of the word root/combining form in the space provided.

	Word Root	Definition
1.	aque/o	_____
2.	blephar/o	_____
3.	acous/o	_____
4.	conjunctiv/o	_____
5.	cor/o	_____
6.	audi/o	_____
7.	corne/o	_____
8.	cycl/o	_____
9.	audit/o	_____
10.	dacry/o	_____
11.	ir/o	_____
12.	auricul/o	_____
13.	irid/o	_____
14.	kerat/o	_____
15.	lacrim/o	_____
16.	ocul/o	_____
17.	cochle/o	_____
18.	ophthalm/o	_____
19.	mastoid/o	_____
20.	opt/o	_____
21.	myring/o	_____
22.	optic/o	_____
23.	ot/o	_____
24.	pupil/o	_____
25.	staped/o	_____
26.	retin/o	_____
27.	tympan/o	_____
28.	scler/o	_____

	Word Root	**Definition**
29.	uve/o	_____
30.	vitre/o	_____

Name _____ Date _____ Errors _____

Test 13B   Identifying Components of the Eye

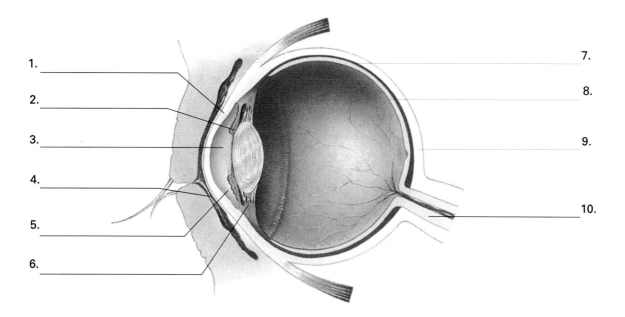

1. _____
2. _____
3. _____
4. _____
5. _____
6. _____

7. _____
8. _____
9. _____

10. _____

Chapter 13   Special Senses   **207**

Name _____ Date _____ Errors _____

Test 13B Instructor's Answers: Components of the Eye

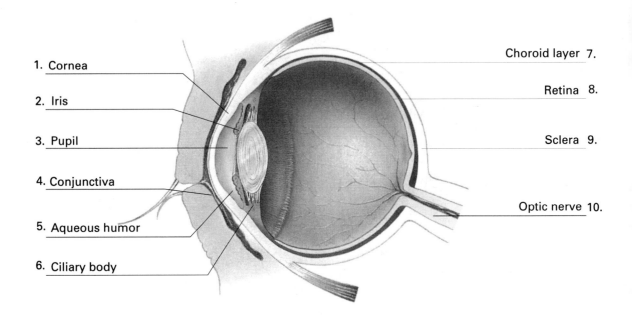

Name _____ Date _____ Errors _____

Test 13C   Identifying Components of the Ear

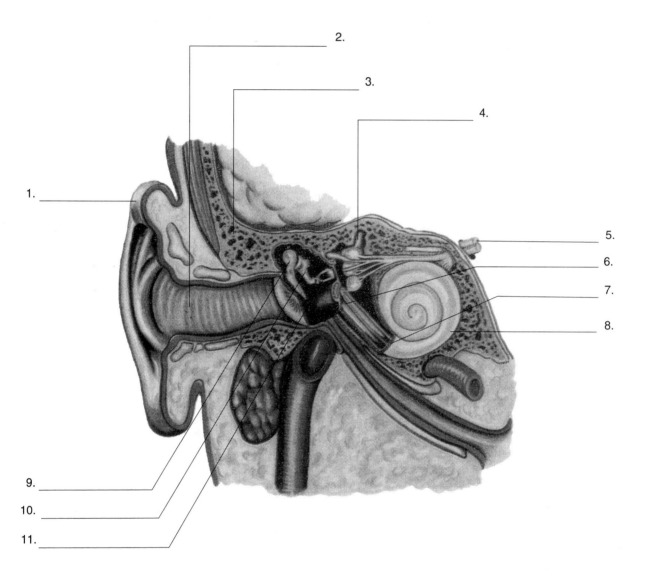

1. _____
2. _____
3. _____
4. _____
5. _____
6. _____
7. _____
8. _____
9. _____
10. _____
11. _____

Name _____ Date _____ Errors _____

Test 13C Instructor's Answers: Components of the Ear

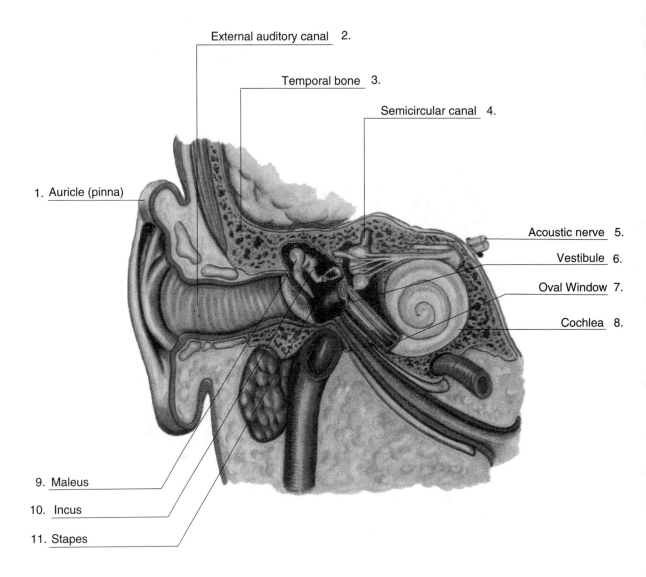

1. Auricle (pinna)
2. External auditory canal
3. Temporal bone
4. Semicircular canal
5. Acoustic nerve
6. Vestibule
7. Oval Window
8. Cochlea
9. Maleus
10. Incus
11. Stapes

Name _____ Date _____ Errors _____

Test 13D Building Words for the Special Senses

Using prefixes and/or suffixes create a medical term for the word roots/combining form listed below.

	Word Root	**New Term**	**Definition**
1.	aque/o		
2.	blephar/o		
3.	acous/o		
4.	conjunctiv/o		
5.	cor/o		
6.	audi/o		
7.	corne/o		
8.	cycl/o		
9.	audit/o		
10.	dacry/o		
11.	ir/o		
12.	auricul/o		
13.	irid/o		
14.	kerat/o		
15.	lacrim/o		
16.	ocul/o		
17.	cochle/o		
18.	ophthalm/o		
19.	mastoid/o		
20.	opt/o		
21.	myring/o		
22.	optic/o		
23.	ot/o		
24.	pupil/o		
25.	staped/o		
26.	retin/o		
27.	tympan/o		
28.	scler/o		

	Word Root	New Term	Definition
29.	uve/o		
30.	vitre/o		

Name _____ Date _____ Errors _____

Test 13E Defining Pathology Relating to the Special Senses

Write the definition for the term in the space provided.

1. cataract _____
2. chalazion _____
3. diabetic retinopathy _____
4. ectropion _____
5. entropion _____
6. glaucoma _____
7. hordeolum _____
8. keratitis _____
9. macular degeneration _____
10. retinal detachment _____
11. retinitis pigmentosa _____
12. strabismus _____
13. trachoma _____
14. acoustic neuroma _____
15. anacusis _____
16. Meniere's disease _____
17. otitis media _____
18. presbyacusis _____

Name _____ Date _____ Errors _____

Test 13F   Defining Disorders Relating to the Special Senses

Write the definition for the term in the space provided.

1. achromatopsia _____
2. astigmatism _____
3. blepharitis _____
4. blepharochalasis _____
5. conjunctivitis _____
6. esotropia _____
7. exophthalmus _____
8. exotropia _____
9. hemianopia _____
10. hyperopia _____
11. myopia _____
12. nystagmus _____
13. presbyopia _____

Name _____ Date _____ Errors _____

Test 13G Defining Procedures and Diagnostic Tests for the Special Senses

Write the definition for the term in the space provided.

1. fluorescein angiography _____
2. laser surgery _____
3. slit-lamp microscope _____
4. vitrectomy _____
5. color vision test _____
6. gonioscopy _____
7. keratometry _____
8. ophthalmoscopy _____
9. Snellen chart _____
10. tonometry _____
11. visual acuity test _____
12. mastoid antrotomy _____
13. myringoplasty _____
14. myringotomy _____
15. otoplasty _____
16. otoscopy _____
17. stapedectomy _____
18. tympanoplasty _____
19. audiogram _____
20. audiometric _____
21. falling test _____
22. mastoid _____
23. otoscopy _____
24. Rinne and Weber tuning-fork tests _____
25. tympanometry _____

Name _____ Date _____ Errors _____

Test 13H Defining Abbreviations for the Special Senses

Write the definition for the term in the space provided.

1. Acc. _____
2. ARMD _____
3. Astigm. _____
4. c.gl. _____
5. cyl. _____
6. D _____
7. DVA _____
8. ECCE _____
9. EM _____
10. EOM _____
11. ICCE _____
12. IOL _____
13. IOP _____
14. L & A _____
15. LE _____
16. MY _____
17. NVA _____
18. OD _____
19. Ophth. _____
20. OS _____
21. OU _____
22. PERLA _____
23. RE _____
24. REM _____
25. s. gl. _____
26. SMD _____
27. VA _____
28. VF _____
29. + _____

30. -
31. AC
32. AD
33. AS
34. AU
35. BC
36. dB
37. ENT
38. EENT
39. OM
40. Oto
41. PE tube
42. UCHD

14

Special Topics

Learning Objectives

Most of the word roots/combining form and abbreviations discussed in this chapter have been covered in previous chapters. Terminology that has not been covered elsewhere in this instructor's manual is covered in this review section.

VOCABULARY TERMINOLOGY

Note. You may wish to use Test 14A to evaluate students' knowledge of vocabulary terms relating to the special topics.

bite-wing x-ray	dental hygienist
endodontics	oral surgery
orthodontics	pedodontics
periodontics	prosthodontics
airway	artificial ventilation
basic life support	blood pressure
crash cart	defibrillator
coronary care unit (CCU)	emergency department
emergency medical technician	intensive care unit (ICU)
residency	stabilize
trauma	triage
vital signs	acute illness
adaptive equipment	aging
ambulate	anxiety
assisted living	chronic disease
developmentally disabled	elder abuse
long term care facility	nursing home
occupational therapy	physical therapy
restorative care	senile
terminal illness	diagnostic
radiation	radioactive
radiography	radioisotope
radiopaque	roentgen
body mechanics	rehabilitation

219

COMMON DENTAL DISORDERS

Note. You may wish to use Test 14B to assess students' understanding of terminology relating to common dental disorders.

dental abscess
gingivitis
impacted wisdom tooth
periodontal disease
plaque

dental caries
gum disease
malocclusion
periodontitis
pyorrhea

PROCEDURES

Note. You may wish to use Test 14C to evaluate students' knowledge of terminology relating to procedures.

intubation
cardiopulmonary resuscitation
finger spelling
speech reading
bridge
denture
root canal
Heimlich maneuver

tourniquet
American Sign Language (ASL)
Signing Exact English (SEE-2)
sign language
crown
implant
first aid

PRONUNCIATION GUIDE: SPECIAL TOPICS

Dental Specialties

endodontist (en do DON tist)
forensic dentist (for EN sik/ dentist)
orthodontist (or tho DON tist)
pedodontist (pe do DON tist)
periodontist (per e oh DON tist)

Types of Teeth

bicuspid (bi KUS pid)
canines (ka NINZ)
cuspid (KUS pid)
deciduous (de SID u us)
incisors (in SI zorz)

General Vocabulary for Dentistry

dental hygienist (denTAL/ hi JE nist)
endodontics (en do DON tiks)
orthodontia (or tho DON she ah)

pedodontics (pe do DON tiks)
periodontics (per e oh DON tiks)
prosthodontics (pros tho DON tiks)

Common Disorders and Pathology Relating to Dentistry

abscess (AB ses)
caries (KAR eez)
gingivitis (jin ji VI tis)
malocclusion (mal oh KLOU shun)
peridontal disease (per e oh DON tal/ di ZEZ)
periodontitis (per e oh don TI tis)
plaque (PLAK)
pyorrhea (pi oh RE ah)

General Vocabulary Relating to Emegency Medicine

artificial ventilation (artificial ventilation)
crepitation (krep ih TA shun)
defibrillator (de fib re LA tor)
Heimlich maneuver (HEIM lik/ man NOO ver)
intubation (in tu BAY shun)
tourniquet (TOOR ni ket)
trauma (TRAW ma)
triage (tre AZH)

Emergency Conditions

amputation (am pu TA shun)
anaphylactic shock (an ah fi LAK tik/ shock)
apnea (ap NE ah)
asphyxia (as FIK se ah)
epiglottitis (ep ih glot I tis)
epilepsy (EP ih lep se)
epistaxis (ep ih STAK sis)
hemorrhage (HEM eh rij)
pneumothorax (nu mo THO raks)

Procedures and Aids for the Hearing Impaired

cochlear implant (KOK le ar/ implant)
polyethylene tube (pol e ETH ih leen/ tube)
stapedectomy (sta pe DEK to me)

Diagnostic and Laboratory Tests for the Hearing Impaired

audiogram (AW de o gram)
audiometer (aw de OM e ter)
mastoid x-ray (MAS toyd/ x-ray)

General Vocabulary of Nuclear Medicine, Radiology, and Radiation Therapy

diagnostic (di ag NOS tik)
electron (e LEK tron)
Geiger counter (GUY ger/ counter)
radiation (ra de AH shun)
radioactive (ra de oh AK tiv)
radium (RE de um)
radiography (ra de OG ra fe)
radioisotope (ra de oh I so top)
radiologist (ra de OL oh jist)
radiopaque (re de oh PAKE)
roentgen (RENT gen)
roentgenologist (rent gen OL oh jist)

Procedures and Diagnostic Tests Relating to Nuclear Medicine, Radiology, and Radiation Therapy

angiocardiography (an je oh kar de OG ra fe)
angiogram (AN je oh gram)
angiography (an je OG ra fe)
aortography (a or TOG ra fe)
arteriography (ar te re OG ra fe)
barium (BA re um)
brachytherapy (brak e THER ah pe)
bronchography (brong KOG ra fe)
cholangiogram (ko LAN je oh gram)
cholecystogram (ko le SIS to gram)
cyclotron (SI klo tron)
echoencephalogram (ek oh en SEF ah lo gram)
echography (ek OG ra fe)
fluroscopy (floo or OS ko pe)
irradiation (ih ra de A shun)
lymphangiography (lim fan je OG ra fe)
mammography (mam OG ra fe)
myelogram (MI eh lo gram)
sonogram (SO no gram)
thermography (ther MOG ra fe)
ultrasound (ul tra SOND)

General Vocabulary for Oncology

benign (be NINE)
carcinogenic (kar SIN oh jen ik)
chemotherapy (ke mo THER ah pe)
encapsulated (en KAP su lat ed)
invasive (in VA sive)
malignant (ma LIG nant)
leukemia (loo KE me ah)
leukoplakia (loo ko PLA ke ah)
lymphoma (lim FO ma)
neuroblastoma (nu ro blas TO ma)
malignant melanoma (malignant/ mel ah NO ma)
medulloblastoma (me dul oh blas TO ma)
metastasis (me TAS ta sis)
multiple myeloma (multiple/ mi e LO ma)
nephrosarcoma (nef ro SAR ko ma)
retinoblastoma (ret ih no blas TO ma)
sarcoma (sar KO ma)

Procedures and Treatment Relating to Oncology

biopsy (BI op se)
chemotherapy (ke mo THER ah pe)
cryosurgery (kri oh SER jer e)
cytologic testing (si to LOG ik/ testing)
hyperplasia (hi per PLA ze ah)
immunotherapy (im u no THER ah pe)
laparotomy (lap ar OT o me)
morbidity (mor BID eh te)
mortality (mor TAL eh te)
mutation (mu TA shun)
neoplasm (NE oh plazm)
oncogenic (ong ko JEN ik)
palliative therapy (PAL e ah tiv/ therapy)
protocol (PRO to kol)
remission (re MISH un)

Pathology Relating to Oncology

adenoma (ad e NO ma)
adenocarcinoma (ad e no kar SIN oh ma)
astrocytoma (as tro si TO ma)
basal cell carcinoma (basal/ cell/ kar si NO ma)
Burkitt's lymphoma (Burkitt's/lim FO ma)
chondrosarcoma (kon dro sar KO ma)

fibrosarcoma (fi bro sar KO ma)
glioblastoma (gli oh blas TO ma)
glioma (gli O ma)
hypernephroma (hi per ne FRO ma)

General Vocabulary for Physical Therapy

circumduction (ser kum DUK shun)
dorsiflexion (DOR se flek shun)
eversion (e VER shun)
flexion (FLEK shun)
gait (GATE)
physiatrist (fiz e AT rist)
pronation (pro NA shun)
rehabilitation (re ha bil ih TA shun)
supination (su pin A shun)

Disorders and Pathology Requiring Physical Therapy

amputation (am pu TA shun)
arthritis (ar THRI tis)
bursitis (bur SI tis)
cerebral palsy (SER e bral / PAWL ze)
multiple sclerosis (multiple/ skle RO sis)
muscular dystrophy (MUS ku lar/ DIS tro fe)
osteoporosis (os te oh por O sis)
paraplegia (par a PLE je ah)
Parkinson's disease (Parkinson's disease)
poliomyelitis (pol e oh mi el I tis)
quadriplegia (kwod ri PLE je ah)
rheumatoid arthritis (ROO ma toid/ ar THRI tis)
tendonitis (TEN dun I tis)

Treatments and Procedures Relating to Physical Therapy

debridement (da bred MONT)
electromyogram (e lek tro MI oh gram)
hydrotherapy (hi dro THER ah pe)
paraffin bath (PAR ah fin/ bath)
percussion (PER kush un)
postural drainage with clapping (POS tu ral/drainage/with/clapping)
short-wave diathermy (short-wave/ DI a ther me)
thermotherapy (ther mo THER ah pe)
traction (TRAK shun)
ultraviolet radiation (ul tra VI o let/ ra de A shun)

Name _____ Date _____ Errors _____

Test 14A Defining Vocabulary Terms Relating to Special Topics

Write the definition for the term in the space provided.

1. bite-wing x-ray _____
2. dental hygienist _____
3. endodontics _____
4. oral surgery _____
5. orthodontics _____
6. pedodontics _____
7. periodontics _____
8. prosthodontics _____
9. airway _____
10. artificial ventilation _____
11. basic life support _____
12. blood pressure _____
13. crash cart _____
14. defibrillator _____
15. coronary care unit (CCU) _____
16. emergency department _____
17. emergency medical technician _____
18. intensive care unit (ICU) _____
19. residency _____
20. stabilize _____
21. trauma _____
22. triage _____
23. vital signs _____
24. acute illness _____
25. adaptive equipment _____
26. aging _____
27. ambulate _____
28. anxiety _____
29. assisted living _____

30. chronic disease _____
31. developmentally disabled _____
32. elder abuse _____
33. long-term care facility _____
34. nursing home _____
35. occupational therapy _____
36. physical therapy _____
37. restorative care _____
38. senile _____
39. terminal illness _____
40. diagnostic _____
41. radiation _____
42. radioactive _____
43. radiography _____
44. radioisotope _____
45. radiopaque _____
46. roentgen _____
47. body mechanics _____
48. rehabilitation _____

Name _____ Date _____ Errors _____

Test 14B Defining Terms Relating to Common Dental Disorders

Write the definition for the term in the space provided.

1. dental abscess _____
2. dental caries _____
3. gingivitis _____
4. gum disease _____
5. impacted wisdom tooth _____
6. malocclusion _____
7. periodontal disease _____
8. periodontitis _____
9. plaque _____
10. pyorrhea _____

Name _____ Date _____ Errors _____

Test 14C Defining Terms Relating to Procedures

Write the definition for the term in the space provided.

1. intubation _____
2. tourniquet _____
3. cardiopulmonary resuscitation _____
4. American Sign Language (ASL) _____
5. finger spelling _____
6. Signing Exact English (SEE-2) _____
7. speech reading _____
8. sign language _____
9. bridge _____
10. crown _____
11. denture _____
12. implant _____
13. root canal _____
14. first aid _____
15. Heimlich maneuver _____

Test Forms

Name _____ Date _____ Errors _____

Write the pronunciation of each medical term in the blank next to the term. Do this by breaking apart the term into its syllables. Circle the syllable on which the emphasis is placed.

Medical Term   **Pronunciation**

1. _____   _____
2. _____   _____
3. _____   _____
4. _____   _____
5. _____   _____
6. _____   _____
7. _____   _____
8. _____   _____
9. _____   _____
10. _____   _____
11. _____   _____
12. _____   _____
13. _____   _____
14. _____   _____
15. _____   _____
16. _____   _____
17. _____   _____
18. _____   _____
19. _____   _____
20. _____   _____
21. _____   _____
22. _____   _____
23. _____   _____

Name _____ Date _____ Errors _____

Break apart the medical term into its word parts. Give a brief definition for the word part(s).

	Word	Word Part(s)	Definition of Word Part(s)
1.			
2.			
3.			
4.			
5.			
6.			
7.			
8.			
9.			
10.			
11.			
12.			
13.			
14.			
15.			
16.			
17.			
18.			
19.			
20.			
21.			
22.			
23.			
24.			
25.			

Name _____ **Date** _____ **Errors** _____

Spelling Test

1. _____
2. _____
3. _____
4. _____
5. _____
6. _____
7. _____
8. _____
9. _____
10. _____
11. _____
12. _____
13. _____
14. _____
15. _____
16. _____
17. _____
18. _____
19. _____
20. _____
21. _____
22. _____
23. _____
24. _____
25. _____

Name _____ **Date** _____ **Errors** _____

Spelling and Definition Test

Spell Term   **Define Term**

1. _____   _____
2. _____   _____
3. _____   _____
4. _____   _____
5. _____   _____
6. _____   _____
7. _____   _____
8. _____   _____
9. _____   _____
10. _____   _____
11. _____   _____
12. _____   _____
13. _____   _____
14. _____   _____
15. _____   _____
16. _____   _____
17. _____   _____
18. _____   _____
19. _____   _____
20. _____   _____
21. _____   _____
22. _____   _____
23. _____   _____
24. _____   _____
25. _____   _____